From Iraq
to
Armageddon

The Final Showdown Approaches

Keith Intrater

Destiny Image® Publishers, Inc.
P.O. Box 310
Shippensburg, PA 17257-0310

"Speaking to the Purposes of God for This Generation
and for the Generations to Come"

ISBN 0-7684-2186-1
(formerly published as 1-56043-041-9)

5 6 7 8 9 10 / 09 08 07 06

For Worldwide Distribution
Printed in the U.S.A.

This book and all other Destiny Image, Revival Press, MercyPlace, Fresh Bread, Destiny Image Fiction, and Treasure House books are available at Christian bookstores and distributors worldwide.

To place a book order, call toll-free: 1-800-722-6774.
For more information on foreign distributors, call 717-532-3040.
Or reach us on the Internet:
www.destinyimage.com

CONTENTS

CHAPTER 1

THE SIGNS OF THE TIMES

The times are urgent. The end of the age is upon us. The pressure is mounting. There are crises all around us and all over the world. It seems like the world just can't take it anymore.

And yet this is just the beginning of the conflicts and difficulties.

Matthew 24:6-8

You will hear of wars and rumors of wars. See that you are not troubled; for all these things must come to pass, but the end is not yet.

For nation will rise against nation, and kingdom against kingdom. And there will be famines, pestilences, and earthquakes in various places.

All these are the beginning of sorrows.

The entire world looks as if it is going through birth pangs. Even the earth itself is groaning as if in labor.

Romans 8:22

For we know that the whole creation groans and labors with birth pangs together until now.

Despite the difficulties of the times we live in, Yeshua (Jesus) tells us not to be afraid. Everything that is happening is part of a plan, which ultimately has a good ending. He likens these tribulations to the birth pangs of a woman in labor (see Jn. 16:21). Despite the horrible pains of giving birth, a woman is overjoyed at the prospect of the new child coming into the world. As soon as that child is born, she forgets the difficulty of her labor.

The Sandwich

So what is the great new thing that we are to look forward to?

The Bible begins and ends with a beautiful picture of paradise. In the beginning we have the Garden of Eden (see Gen. 1–3). At the end we see a picture of paradise restored, the "heavenly Jerusalem," with Heaven and earth living in perfect harmony (see Rev. 20–22).

So the story of the Bible as a whole is somewhat like a sandwich. The piece of bread at the beginning and at the end is a beautiful time of peace and prosperity. There will be such happiness that no one will even shed a tear from sorrow.

Revelation 21:4

And God will wipe away every tear from their eyes; there shall be no more death, nor sorrow, nor crying. There shall be no more pain, for the former things have passed away.

Unfortunately, most of the story between those two pictures of paradise is filled with sorrow and sin. The meat between the two pieces of bread is bitter and tough. Human history is filled with conflict and pain, not only between men and men, but also between men and God.

That Great and Terrible Day

The conflicts of human history are building up toward one final conflict. That conflict is a great war. That war is sometimes referred to as Armageddon, the battle of Gog and Magog, or the Apocalypse. The tribulations and conflicts of our time will increase steadily in their intensity until that final clash.

It is during the great end-times war that the Messiah will come. Yeshua will intervene, stop the war, bring judgment to the wicked, and establish the period of Messianic peace upon the earth. The second coming of Yeshua is the focal point of all the prophecies of the endtimes. It is the main event. Because of the war and because of the judgment, this event is referred to by the Hebrew prophets as:

Joel 2:31 KJV

"the great and terrible day of the Lord [YHVH]. *"*

In terms of biblical history, the period of time in which we now live may be seen as a plain between two mountain peaks. The mountain peak behind us is the crucifixion of Yeshua, and the mountain peak in front of us is the Second Coming. With each day that passes, we come closer to that second peak—closer to that great and terrible day of YHVH, the day of the coming of Messiah.

At the cross, Yeshua came as the sacrificial lamb to take away the sins of the world. At the Second Coming, He will appear as a roaring lion to punish those who have rebelled against God. At Mount Calvary Yeshua offered us grace. When He returns to the Mount of Olives, He will execute justice.

The Double Anointing

The primary text that Yeshua used to preach from while He was here on the earth was Isaiah 61. This is a passage that speaks of preaching the good news of God's grace.

Isaiah 61:1-2a

The Spirit of the Lord God is upon Me, because the Lord has anointed Me to preach good tidings to the poor; He has sent Me to heal the brokenhearted, to proclaim liberty to the captives, and the opening of the prison to those who are bound;

To proclaim the acceptable year of the Lord...

It is interesting to note that in the first century when Yeshua preached, He ended His text in the middle of verse 2. The second half of the verse continues:

Isaiah 61:2b

...and the day of vengeance of our God.

The preaching of the gospel has a twofold anointing. Yeshua concentrated on the aspects of forgiveness and healing in the first century because, according to the plan of God, it was the time for Him to be crucified to offer atonement and salvation to man. (This came as a surprise to the Jewish people of the first century, including His own disciples, since they were expecting the Messiah to come as a conquering king.)

However, as we approach the Second Coming, the second half of the Isaiah 61 passage becomes more urgent. The gospel needs to be preached in the light of the Second Coming. There is a powerful prophetic anointing that comes with the second half of the message, just as much as that which comes with the first. Yeshua is anointed as both the suffering servant and the conquering king.

The Timing

The dispensation of time in which we now live, where the gospel is being preached around the world, occurs roughly at the same time as the great exile of the Jewish people to all the nations of the world. One generation after the crucifixion of Yeshua, Jewish people were sent into exile (A.D. 70). Now that we are in the generation preceding the Second Coming, the Jewish people are being regathered to their land.

This is not a coincidence.

As we look at the rest of Isaiah 61, we will see that the passage deals primarily with the restoration of Israel as a nation. Yes, the passage deals with executing judgment, establishing justice, and bringing joy to the earth. However, those elements are given in the context of the restoration of Israel.

Isaiah 61:3-7
To console those who mourn in Zion...

They shall rebuild the old ruins...and they shall repair the ruined cities, the desolations of many generations.

Strangers shall stand and feed your flocks...

You shall eat the riches of the Gentiles...

Therefore in their land they shall possess double.

The restoration of Israel is the overall context of Isaiah chapters 60–62. When Yeshua was raised from the dead, His disciples expected Him to bring the restoration of Israel immediately, and then through that restoration to bring peace to the rest of the world. Before He ascended into Heaven, He taught them for 40 days about the Kingdom of God. They responded:

Acts 1:6
Lord, will You at this time restore the kingdom to Israel?

Yeshua replied that it was not the time for the restoration of Israel. There would be a long period first in which the gospel would be preached to all the nations of the world, and then would come the time for the establishment of the Messianic kingdom on earth. The establishment of the Messianic kingdom on earth takes place at the end of the preaching of the gospel all over the world.

Acts 1:7-8
It is not for you to know the times or seasons which the Father has put in His own authority.

But you shall receive power when the Holy Spirit has come upon you; and you shall be witnesses to Me in Jerusalem, and in all Judea and Samaria, and to the end of the earth.

Since the Messianic kingdom on earth is connected with the restoration of Israel, and since the Messianic kingdom comes at the end of the gospel era, it is logical that the nation of Israel be restored at the time when the gospel era approaches its end.

Yeshua's disciples missed the fact that the gentile nations are to take part in establishing the Messianic kingdom on the earth. The message of salvation was to come from the Jews to the nations (see Jn. 4:22), but then the believers in every nation were to rise up and take part in establishing the kingdom. Establishing the kingdom on earth would mean bringing Jesus back. Since Jesus (Yeshua) was to come back to the nation of Israel, obviously the nation of Israel would have to be restored as part of the process leading up to the Second Coming.

The Two Prerequisites

There are two great prerequisites for the second coming of Yeshua. The first is world evangelism:

Matthew 24:14

This gospel of the kingdom will be preached in all the world as a witness to all the nations, and then the end will come.

The Kingdom of God is for all people. Before the kingdom can come to earth, the gospel invitation must be offered to every person. This is why world evangelism must be a priority for all of us. We need to share the gospel everywhere. We need to pray for everyone to be saved. And we need to give money toward evangelistic and apostolic missions.

The second prerequisite has to do more specifically with revival in Israel. Yeshua turned to His own Jewish brethren who were rejecting Him in the first century and said:

Matthew 23:37-39

O Jerusalem, Jerusalem, the one who kills the prophets and stones those who are sent to her! How often I wanted to gather your children together, as a hen gathers her chicks under her wings, but you were not willing!

See! Your house is left to you desolate;

For I say to you, you shall see Me no more till you say, "Blessed is He who comes in the name of the Lord!"

Here Yeshua predicted the destruction of the temple and the dispersion of the Jewish people when He said, "Your house is left to you desolate."

The Gospel and the Dispersion

When Yeshua said that He wished to "gather" the Jewish people to Him, He was referring to personal salvation through faith, and to regathering the exiles to Israel from the four corners of the earth. Had the Jewish religious leaders accepted Yeshua, there would have been no need for the two-thousand-year exile.

Had the Jewish people as a nation taken it upon themselves to fulfill their priestly calling by presenting the gospel of the kingdom to all the nations, there would have been no need for the exile. Someone once said, if you don't take Acts 1:8—to go out to spread the gospel around the world; you get Acts 8:1—in which the early believers in Jerusalem were scattered throughout the regions because of persecution. Either way, whether through cooperation or constraint, the purposes of God will be fulfilled.

The Jewish people were dispersed in exile in a parallel manner to which the gospel was spread around the world. As the Jews were exiled, so were the first-century Messianic apostles and evangelists dispersed with them. While the nation as a whole was being punished, the Messianic remnant brought blessing and salvation to the Gentiles.

So the gospel went with the Jews, and the Jews went with the gospel. For the past two thousand years, most of the Jewish people have lived in exile in "Christian" nations, first in Europe, then in America. At first this exile allowed for the gospel to come to the Gentiles. Later it was designed by God as an opportunity for Christians to bring the gospel back to the Jewish people.

Anti-Semitism and the Exile

Therefore, anti-Semitism and persecution of the Jews at the hands of so-called Christian nations was the exact opposite of the purpose of God. In fact, it makes Him angry. Here is God's evaluation of anti-Semitism and the exile:

Zechariah 1:14-15

I am zealous for Jerusalem and for Zion with great zeal.

I am exceedingly angry with the nations at ease; for I was a little angry, and they helped—but with an evil intent.

The King James translates that last phrase as "they helped forward the affliction." The Hebrew is *azru l'ra'ah*, which means "they helped for evil." The exile of the Jewish people was a punishment from God for our sins and for rejecting Yeshua (see Lk. 19:44). However, the ill treatment of the Jews at the hands of the Gentiles during the exile added extra punishment that was contrary to the will of God.

How Much More Their Restoration

Amazingly, God used His punishment on the Jewish people to bring the message of salvation to the gentile nations. In return, His plan was that they would bring the gospel back to the Jews, and then together, the international church and the restored remnant of Israel would give birth to the Messianic kingdom on the earth.

Romans 11:11-12, 15
Through their fall, to provoke them to jealousy, salvation has come to the Gentiles.

Now if their fall is riches for the world, and their failure riches for the Gentiles, how much more their fullness!

For if their being cast away is the reconciling of the world, what will their acceptance be but life from the dead?

The gospel of salvation is a universal message of forgiveness available to every human being. It has no connection to time, place, or ethnic origin. That's why there was no hindrance to the spread of the gospel when Israel was dispersed as a nation. On the contrary, it even helped to some degree, by removing political or cultural stumbling blocks.

However, there is more to come. When Yeshua returns, He will bring the resurrection of the dead and peace on earth. When He returns, He will have to return to a specific place and at a specific time. The Messianic kingdom will have a real society with real people. In that context, the restoration of the nation of Israel has significance.

Yeshua was crucified as "King of the Jews" (Jn. 19:19). He was ridiculed on the cross for being "The King of Israel" (Mk. 15:32). Yeshua has not yet fulfilled His calling as the King of the Jews. In the message of universal forgiveness, the role of the nation of Israel has less importance. However, in the message of the Messianic kingdom—with the Second Coming, the resurrection of the dead, and the era of peace on earth, the nation of Israel does have an important role to play.

Yeshua was crucified as the King of Israel, and He will return to conquer as the King of Israel. Yeshua said that He would not come back until the Jews in Israel were ready to receive Him (see Mt. 23:39). But they cannot receive Him if they are not there. Before there can be a revival in Israel, there must be people in Israel. Before the spiritual kingdom can be restored to Israel, the physical nation of Israel must be brought back into existence.

Jewish Believers in Yeshua

Over the past hundred years God has been bringing the Jewish people back to the land. More recently there has been the spread of faith in Yeshua among Jewish people both in Israel and around the world. Again, the timing is not a coincidence. World evangelism and the restoration of Israel are part of the process that leads up to the Second Coming. The link between world evangelism and the restoration of Israel are the Jewish people who have become believers in Yeshua.

I can remember thinking, in the late 1970s when I came to faith in Yeshua, that I must be the only Jewish person in the world who believes in Jesus. Many of us who were part of those first waves of Jewish people coming to know the Lord felt the same way. Without knowing it, we were fulfilling prophecies from the New Testament that were written almost two thousand years before we were born.

Luke 21:24
And they will fall by the edge of the sword, and be led away captive into all nations. And Jerusalem will be trampled by Gentiles until the times of the Gentiles are fulfilled.

Here Yeshua again prophesied of the coming destruction of Jerusalem and the exile of the Jewish people. Yet this was also part of His prophecies about the endtimes, which predicted that Jerusalem would one day come back into the hands of the Jews.

After the destruction of Israel as a nation, the gospel was to go forth to the gentile nations. As the time of the gospel to the Gentiles would start to come to an end, the Jewish people would be regathered to Israel and the city of Jerusalem recaptured.

At that time, Jewish people would start to believe in Yeshua again. Paul stated:

Romans 11:25b-26a
Blindness in part has happened to Israel until the fullness of the Gentiles has come in.

And so all Israel will be saved.

If we compare Yeshua's words in Luke 21 with Paul's words in Romans 11, we find that at the time of the "fullness of the Gentiles" these three events would coincide: Jerusalem would be recaptured by the Jews; Jewish people would begin to believe in Yeshua again; and the spread of the gospel to the nations would come into its final stages.

Jerusalem was recaptured in 1967. Since that time, true to the prophecies, Jewish people, independently and spontaneously, both in Israel and around the world, have started believing in Yeshua. Since that time as well, there has been an expansion of world evangelism and a greater outpouring of the Holy Spirit.

The Double Invitation

Those two great prerequisites—world evangelism and revival in Israel—should be deep burdens upon our hearts. They should be powerful sources of motivation for us as we seek to serve the Lord.

Both world evangelism and revival in Israel will bring us to the second coming of Yeshua. Even though Yeshua is a conquering king, He is still a gentleman. He will only come back when He is invited. The invitation for Him to return is two-sided: It comes from both the international Church and the remnant of Israel.

Revelation 22:20b

Even so, come [Maranatha]*, Lord Jesus!*

The international community of faith, made up of the remnant of true believers in every nation, will cry out, "Maranatha!"

Matthew 23:39

You shall see Me no more till you say, 'Blessed is He who comes in the name of the Lord [Baruch haba b'shem adonai]*!"*

The restored remnant of Jewish believers in Yeshua in the endtimes will cry out, "Baruch HaBa." At this dual invitation Yeshua will return. Just as there was cooperation in the negative between the Jewish religious leaders and the Roman military leaders to crucify Yeshua, so will there be a positive cooperation between Jewish and gentile believers to invite Yeshua back.

God's Clock

Yeshua told us that we should try to understand the timing of spiritual events. He said we should know how to "discern the signs of the times"

(Mt. 16:3). The fact that Israel has become a nation and that Jewish people are already starting to believe in Yeshua is a sign that we are getting close to the Second Coming.

Matthew 24:32
Now learn this parable from the fig tree: When its branch has al-ready become tender and puts forth leaves, you know that sum-mer is near.

The fig tree is the symbol of the nation of Israel. The summer is the end of the age. The word "summer" in Hebrew is the same root as the word for "end." There is a play on words here that Yeshua is repeating from Amos 8:2. The leaves on the fig tree are the beginning of the spiritual restoration of Israel. And those leaves have already started to blossom. This is a sign— a kind of clock from God—to let us know that the time of the kingdom re-ally is at hand.

Chapter 2

Two Armies

While there are many prophecies about the endtimes, there are two passages that give us a clear picture of the actual event of the Second Coming—one in the Old Testament (see Zech. 14) and one in the New (see Rev. 19). Both of them describe a great battle. The version in Zechariah sees the battle from an earthly perspective, with the nations gathered against Israel. The version in Revelation views the same scene from a heavenly perspective, as an angelic battle.

In order to understand correctly the Second Coming, we need to see these two pictures as describing the same event. When the two descriptions match one another in our thoughts, then we will know that we have gotten the picture right. Let's look at the version in the New Testament first:

Revelation 19:11-15

Now I saw heaven opened, and behold a white horse. And He who sat on him was called Faithful and True, and in righteousness He judges and makes war.

His eyes were like a flame of fire, and on His head were many crowns. He had a name written that no one knew except Himself.

He was clothed with a robe dipped in blood, and His name is called The Word of God.

And the armies in heaven, clothed in fine linen, white and clean, followed Him on white horses.

Now out of His mouth goes a sharp sword, that with it He should strike the nations. And He Himself will rule them with a rod of iron. He Himself treads the winepress of the fierceness and wrath of Almighty God.

In this picture we see Yeshua as an angelic figure, or rather, as the commander of the armies of Heaven. He is leading the armies descending out of the sky. While He and His soldiers are perfectly pure, they are also very angry, and in a sense extremely violent. They are executing the wrath and judgment of God. He has come to enforce the authority of God over the nations of the world with a hand of iron.

While the picture of Yeshua is figurative, and while His soldiers are angelic, they are portrayed here as intervening in a real human battle and conquering military forces on the earth. Let's look at it now from the Old Testament view:

> Zechariah 14:2-4,12
> *I will gather all the nations to battle against Jerusalem. The city shall be taken, the houses rifled, and the women ravished. Half of the city shall go into captivity, but the remnant of the people shall not be cut off from the city.*
>
> *Then the Lord will go forth and fight against those nations, as He fights in the day of battle.*
>
> *And in that day His feet will stand on the Mount of Olives, which faces Jerusalem on the east...*
>
> *And this shall be the plague with which the Lord will strike all the people who fought against Jerusalem: Their flesh shall dissolve while they stand on their feet, their eyes shall dissolve in their sockets, and their tongues shall dissolve in their mouths.*

Again we see a picture of a battle with great violence. Of course, the Old Testament does not specifically mention of the name *Yeshua*. He is referred to as YHVH (see Zech. 14:3,12). It also says that His "feet will stand on the Mount of Olives" (Zech.14:4). The description of Him standing on the Mount of Olives clearly points to Yeshua Himself. Yeshua rose into Heaven from the Mount of Olives (see Acts 1:9). When He ascended, the angels told the disciples that Yeshua would return "in the same manner" (Acts 1:11). In other words, we can assume that the same Yeshua who rose into Heaven from the Mount of Olives in Acts 1 will also return to set His feet upon the Mount of Olives as described in Zechariah 14.

Two Pictures

While the version in Zechariah does not specifically mention the name *Yeshua*, the version in Revelation does not specifically mention the city of Jerusalem. For this reason, many Jewish people understand the apocalyptic war as a battle over Jerusalem, but do not see any connection of it with Yeshua. On the other hand, many Christians are aware that Yeshua will return during a supernatural apocalypse, but see no connection with the city of Jerusalem.

In order to get the picture right, you have to see both halves—both Jesus and Jerusalem. The combining of the classic Jewish and Christian views of the coming of the Messiah will give us the complete picture. The division of this picture into two separate viewpoints—one Christian and one Jewish, not connected to one another—is a primary source of confusion concerning the endtimes, whether on the Christian side or the Jewish side.

Quite frankly, both the pictures here are frightening. As amazing as was the grace of Yeshua to forgive sins at His first coming, so will His judgment be astonishing in the punishment of sins at the Second Coming. Both sinful men and satanic angels will be thrown into the lake of fire for eternity (see Rev. 20). Greedy and tyrannical leaders in business, politics, and the military will cry out to the mountains to cover them in order to hide from "the wrath of the Lamb" (Rev. 6:17). God's vengeance will be terrifying.

Two Armies

In ancient Israel there were two armies: the army of the people of Israel and the angelic army of the Lord of Hosts. The word "hosts" in Hebrew is ts'vaot, which simply means "armies." The Jehovah God of ancient Israel was called the Lord of the Armies. In the biblical worldview, angelic battles take place in the heavenlies whenever there are political, religious, or military conflicts here on earth.

When ancient Israel's army went forth to battle, they understood that there was an angelic army accompanying them about ten meters over their heads. It was comparable to today's ground troops being accompanied by a modern air force.

2 Samuel 5:24
When you hear the sound of marching in the tops of the mulberry trees, then you shall advance quickly. For then the Lord will go out before you to strike the camp of the Philistines.

In this case, the angelic army helped King David in a battle against the Philistines. Other godly kings and commanders experienced the same thing. (See also Second Chronicles 14; Joshua 5, 10, Second Kings 19, etc.)

Messianic Soldiers

A special link between the angelic armies and the earthly armies is the young Messianic Jewish men and women who are serving in the Israeli army today. Not only are they soldiers in the IDF (Israeli Defense Forces), but they also have a spiritual connection with the heavenly armies through prayer and faith. Think of the phenomenon of born-again, Spirit-filled young men and women serving in the Israeli army. There is as much written in the Bible about the Israeli army as there is about intercessory prayer or church planting. While the number of Messianic soldiers is still comparatively small, many of them serve in significant roles in battle units, fighting against terrorism.

At one of the fellowships that my wife, Betty, arranged, we hosted about 30 Messianic soldiers for dinner, worship, teaching, and fun. I had the opportunity to share with them the two pictures of the Second Coming as described in Revelation 19 and Zechariah 14. I believe these Messianic soldiers have a special role to play in the conflicts of the endtimes. They are on the front lines of spiritual warfare in the truest sense of the word. Spiritual warfare includes those engaged in intercessory prayer, those involved in preaching the Word of God—and in fact anyone who obeys God in a difficult situation. Spiritual warfare also includes soldiers in the Israeli army, as well as the angels serving in the heavenly army.

At the time of this writing, my two older boys are both serving in the IDF. My daughter and youngest son will also enlist in the near future. We realize that from the year 2000 to the year 2014, at least one of our children will be serving in the Israeli army full time. Dealing with the reality of this extended military experience has helped our family to understand some aspects of the Bible that we had never seen before.

The Israeli army experience forms part of the cultural background of the Bible. In the Old Testament that background is quite real. Consider Abraham's rescue of Lot (see Gen. 14) or David's mighty men (see 2 Sam. 23). In the New Testament it is more figurative, such as in Paul's description of the disciplines of a believer (see 2 Tim. 2) or spiritual warfare (see 2 Cor. 10).

This context of the Israeli army and its spiritual remnant helps to explain some of the prophecies concerning the Second Coming. Zechariah 14 describes an army fighting against the nations who have attacked Israel, while Revelation 19 describes an army fighting against those who have refused to obey the gospel. There seems to be no way to reconcile those two pictures. However, when you realize that among the Israeli soldiers are those who believe in Yeshua, the two pictures begin to be joined together.

These Messianic soldiers form a living bridge between the two aspects of the second coming of Yeshua. In them, the heavenly side and the Israeli side become one. Yeshua is their ultimate commander, both in the military sense and in the spiritual sense. They are an important link to Yeshua as He prepares to return to earth to destroy the forces of evil, both angelic and human. Please take a moment even as you read this to pray for those young Messianic Jewish men and women serving in the Israeli army—for their protection and for the witness of the gospel that they bring to the other soldiers.

The Commander in Chief

For most of us it is difficult to see Yeshua as a military figure. It is easier to picture Him as a kind of "flower child" walking around the Sea of Galilee with long hair, sandals, and a white robe. Kissing babies seems to be more His style than killing enemies.

Yet the picture we see in Revelation states, "His eyes were like a flame of fire" (Rev. 19:12). That flame is a flame of anger. He is fierce and furious. The description of Him stamping and crushing the grapes in the winepress of God's wrath (see Rev. 19:15) is so poetic that we easily miss the blood and gore of that horrible punishment. The description in Zechariah 14:12a states of His enemies that "their flesh shall dissolve while they stand on their feet."

One of the clearest pictures of Yeshua as commander in chief is seen in the confrontation between Joshua and the Angel of the Lord on the eve of the battle of Jericho.

Joshua 5:13-15

And it came to pass, when Joshua was by Jericho, that he lifted his eyes and looked, and behold, a Man stood opposite him with His sword drawn in His hand. And Joshua went to Him and said to Him, "Are You for us or for our adversaries?"

So He said, "No, but as Commander of the army of the Lord I have now come." And Joshua fell on his face to the earth and worshiped, and said to Him, "What does my Lord say to His servant?"

Then the Commander of the Lord's army said to Joshua, "Take your sandal off your foot, for the place where you stand is holy." And Joshua did so.

This heavenly Man is none other than Yeshua Himself, as we see by the fact that Joshua removed His sandals and worshiped Him. The name Joshua and the name Jesus in the Hebrew are the same name, literally "Yehoshua." You could call this a meeting between the big "J" and the little "J."

Yeshua comes to us in different manifestations—as a baby, as a carpenter, as a preacher, as an angel. He often comes "walking on the water" to rescue us. But in this case, He came as the Commander of the army of the Lord. Can you see Him in that role? At the Second Coming, He will certainly be in that role.

Here again we see the two armies, this time with the two commanders. The Israeli army has worth only to the degree that it submits to Yeshua's heavenly army. Joshua submitted to Yeshua, not the other way around. The question was not whether Yeshua was on Israel's side, but whether Israel was on Yeshua's side. So it is today. In Joshua 5, Zechariah 14, and Revelation 19, they are found fighting together.

The commander in chief of the Israeli army is called the "Ramat Kal." When my second son, Freddy, went to enlist, Shaul Mofaz, then Ramat Kal, happened to pay a surprise visit to the incoming soldiers and their parents. Freddy and I were photographed with him, just the three of us. It struck me as being symbolic of turning my son over to the Commander as well as the commander, for his service in the army.

The IDF Standard

I am not saying that everyone in the Israeli army is a godly person—in fact, quite the opposite is true. The IDF has its share of disciplinary problems with drugs, immorality, and insubordination. Nor am I saying that every action of the Israeli army is justified. The army is plagued by mistakes and mismanagement. However, I do claim that as an institution, it is a vehicle of God's authority in the sense that Romans 13:4 states, "For he is God's minister to you for good. But if you do evil, be afraid; for he does not bear the sword in vain; for he is God's minister, an avenger to execute wrath on him who practices evil."

Many of the reports in the international media of so-called "slaughters" by the Israeli army were outright lies and propaganda. I know, from the training our boys have received in the army, how much stress is placed on "weapons purity." Weapons purity is not talking about cleaning the rifle, but about using the weapon only with integrity when necessary for a military objective. The soldiers are taught never to use a weapon to threaten an innocent civilian. In this regard I believe their standards are very high. Do the soldiers always abide by those standards? No. In general, are the standards kept? Yes.

In my wallet I keep a small pamphlet called, "The Spirit of the IDF," which the soldiers are supposed to carry with them at all times. This document states that the IDF is an army submitted to civilian law and order, and that commanders and soldiers alike are required to obey the code of ethics.

The pamphlet also describes the specific character and moral values of the Israeli army, such as faithfulness, respect for human life, commitment to excellence and victory, personal discipline, setting an example, being a professional, and seeing oneself as a representative of the nation of Israel.

Swearing-In Ceremony

Not long ago Betty and I drove down to attend the swearing-in ceremony for one of our boys. To finish this chapter, I include here some of my notes from that event, which we found quite moving:

"Midafternoon. Somewhere in the Negev Desert in southern Israel. Approximately 800 young recruits have completed their first stage of "tiranut" (boot camp) and are about to be sworn in to the Israeli Defense Forces. The sun is hot. The atmosphere is formal and relaxed at the same time. Family members and girlfriends have traveled long hours to see this event.

The loud speaker announces the opening of the ceremony. The new soldiers march in, with their commanders at the head of each unit. The Israeli flag is raised and saluted. An army rabbi comes to the front and reads from Joshua 1:

"Arise, go over this Jordan, you and all this people, to the land which I am giving them—the children of Israel. Every place that the sole of your foot will tread upon I have given you...

No man shall be able to stand before you all the days of your life; as I was with Moses, so I will be with you...

Be strong and of good courage, for to this people you shall [give this land as a possession] *which I swore to their fathers to give them. Only be strong and very courageous..."*

There is something of destiny, of heritage, of history, of faith—
"...the land sworn to your forefathers." A dim echo of the foot-
steps of Abraham and Joshua hover over the ancient hills.

After a few words of encouragement by the senior base commander, the oath of the IDF is read aloud. The recruits are to be
sworn to protect the "moledet" (land of their forefathers), even to
the point of sacrificing their lives if necessary.

At the end of the reading of the oath, the recruits shout out together three times, in the deepest macho tones that their barely
post-adolescent voices can muster, "Ani Nishba" (I swear). They
are entering into a covenant as the patriarchs did with Jehovah,
the God of the tribes of Israel.

Then the recruits prepare to receive their rifles from their unit
commanders. One by one they step forward. They salute. In their
left hand they receive a rifle, and in their right hand they receive
a copy of the Hebrew Bible. Standing before their commander,
they reach over with their right hand and touch the Bible to the
rifle.

The army rabbi returns to the microphone and reads from Isaiah
2:

*"It shall come to pass in the latter days that the mountain of the
Lord's house shall be established...and all nations shall flow to
it...out of Zion shall go forth the law and the word of the Lord
from Jerusalem.*

*He shall judge between the nations, and rebuke many people;
they shall beat their swords into plowshares, and their spears
into pruning hooks; nation shall not lift up sword against nation,
neither shall they learn war anymore."*

The soldiers' task in the IDF is seen as part of the dream of the
prophets to bring the Kingdom of God and peace upon the earth.

The ceremony ends with the singing of the Israeli anthem,
"HaTikvah" (the hope). The words are taken from the "dry
bones" prophecy of Ezekiel 37 about the hope of the nation of Israel to be resurrected and restored after two thousand years of
exile and spiritual death."

The situation is both stirring and heartbreaking. These young men are risking their lives to defend Israel and to fight terrorism. Yet very few of them have received forgiveness of sins and eternal life from Yeshua. They are sinners. They are lost morally and spiritually. Heartbreaking as well is the thought that most of the evangelical Christian community is distanced and unaware of something that is close to the heart of Yeshua.

CHAPTER 3

THE CENTRAL FIGURE

God is a spirit being (see Jn. 4:24).

God Is Spirit

Somehow in His infinite wisdom God decided that He wanted to create physical beings in His image (see Gen. 1:26). He would do this both for the purpose of living inside of them (see Ex. 25:8; 29:46; 1 Cor. 6:16) and for having a relationship with them. He decided and planned all this before He created the world. It was for this purpose that the world was created.

Ephesians 1:4-5

He chose us in Him before the foundation of the world, that we should be holy and without blame before Him in love,

Having predestined us to adoption as sons by Jesus Christ to Himself, according to the good pleasure of His will.

So God, as a spiritual being, wanted to live in a physical world. He wanted to live there by dwelling inside of those human beings that He would create. He wanted to have a relationship with them as well.

God would fulfill this plan in stages. He created two worlds, both a spiritual world (heaven) and a physical world (earth). In those two worlds He created two sets of beings that were made in His image. The angels were His "sons" in the spiritual realm. Human beings were to be His sons in the physical realm.

Since God is a spirit being, the creation started with a spiritual side. The angels were created first. Afterwards, God made Adam, then Eve, and through them He populated the physical earth. Ultimately He planned for both of these worlds to come together in perfect harmony.

Necessary Risks

Of course there were certain risks to this plan. If God made a created being that He planned to raise up to a level of fellowship with Himself, there was the risk of that being falling into *pride*. The first problem with both angels and humans is pride.

The second risk was that if He made a physical world full of beauty and pleasure, His created beings might be tempted toward *lust* when they saw the beauties of creation and felt its pleasures. Lust is the second problem.

The third risk was that in order to give these created beings the option to love Him, God had to give them free will. With that free will, they could choose to love God, but they could also choose not to love God. The choice to reject God's love and authority is what we call *sin*.

So in the very decision to make a physical world with creatures formed in His image, God took the risk of these three inherent problems: *pride*, *lust*, and *sin*.

The Agent

There is a person, the primary agent or messenger from God, whose task is to execute the original plan of God and to overcome the inherent problems. That person is Yeshua, the Messiah, the Son of God. The more one reads the Bible, the more he becomes aware that Yeshua is the central figure of the entire story: not just of the Gospels, but also of the Law, the Prophets and the Epistles.

There are several reasons why Yeshua is the central figure, even though the Father is greater than He (see Jn. 14:28), and even though He submitted under the authority of the Father (see 1 Cor. 15:28).

God coming in

God is a spirit being; yet because He made us as physical creatures for Himself to dwell in, there had to be a way for Him to approach us. There had to be a way for Him to come into our midst, to reveal Himself to us—to manifest His spiritual presence within the physical world.

John 1:1,14,18

In the beginning was the Word, and the Word was with God, and the Word was God.

And the Word became flesh and dwelt among us, and we beheld His glory, the glory as of the only begotten of the Father, full of grace and truth.

No one has seen God at any time. The only begotten Son, who is in the bosom of the Father, He has [made Him known].

Obviously, the best way for God to have approached human creatures for a relationship with Himself was in the form of a human. This was the first role of Yeshua. We may say that we believe in God, but Yeshua is the manifestation of God to us. He is God's offer to have a personal relationship with Him.

Offering forgiveness

When He made us with free will, God knew that there was the likelihood, if not the inevitability, that we would sin. He prepared a means of offering us forgiveness of sins before He even created the world. The crucifixion of Yeshua was inevitable and planned before Creation itself.

Revelation 13:8b

...in the Book of Life of the Lamb slain from the foundation of the world.

While the Roman politicians were motivated to crucify Yeshua out of fear, and the Jewish priests out of jealousy, God Himself had another purpose. God planned the Crucifixion in order to offer human beings forgiveness. Yeshua chose to cooperate with that plan.

Since it was human beings who sinned, the atonement for the sins also had to be done by a human. Therefore it was not the Father who was crucified, but the Son. Yeshua is the agent through whom we receive forgiveness.

Crushing the rebellion

Since God gave us free will, there was the possibility that we would sin. With that same free will, every person still has the option either to turn back to God or to harden himself into a continuing opposition to God's authority.

For those who would be willing to change and choose a relationship with God, Yeshua came to offer forgiveness. However, for those who would stubbornly insist on rebelling, Yeshua came to bring judgment and punishment.

This punishment will take place at the moment of the Second Coming.

2 Thessalonians 1:7b-8

When the Lord [Yeshua] *is revealed from heaven with His mighty angels,*

*In flaming fire taking vengeance on those who do not know God,
and on those who do not obey the gospel...*

Yeshua not only executes the punishment, He is the one who sits as the judge.

Acts 10:42b
*It is He who was ordained by God to be Judge of the living and
the dead.*

Standards of absolute justice require that a person be judged by a peer. It would be impossible for a spirit being, whether it be an angel or God Himself, to be appointed as the judge over men. They have not experienced the same set of conditions that we have, as physical beings with free will in a material world.

John 5:22,27
*The Father judges no one, but has committed all judgment to the
Son.*

*And has given Him authority to execute judgment also, because
He is the Son of Man.*

Yeshua, being a son of man—a son of Adam, a human being—is able to execute righteous judgment on behalf of God. (He is righteous because He is divine; He has jurisdiction because He is human.) Yeshua is the primary agent for the righteous judgment of God.

Pinnacle of man's destiny

God made us so that He could dwell in us and have a relationship with us. However, no human being independently can achieve that highest level of spirituality. Yeshua is not only God coming down to visit man, He is also the leader of the human race rising up into its destiny to become one with God.

Yeshua is the first human being to be filled with the fullness of God.

Colossians 2:9
For in Him dwells all the fullness of the Godhead bodily.

The fullness of this indwelling is not just for Yeshua, but also for us to become complete in Him.

Colossians 2:10a
And you are complete in Him.

Ultimately it is not just for Yeshua to be filled with all the fullness of God, but also for each one of us.

Ephesians 3:19
To know the love of Christ which passes knowledge; that you may be filled with all the fullness of God.

This fullness is for us collectively as the international body of believers (see Eph. 1:23), and also for each of us individually (see Eph. 3:19).

When He breathed His spirit into Adam, God created us with partial divinity (see Gen. 2:7). As we received our physical body through Adam, we will receive our resurrection body through Yeshua. Adam was God's agent to give us our humanity, but Yeshua is God's agent to lead us into the fullness of our divine destiny.

Bridge between Heaven and earth

God is a spiritual being who wanted to create a physical world. He had to create two worlds (spiritual and physical), and then bring them together. The sin of mankind through Adam, and the rebellion of the angels through Satan, caused a split between Heaven and earth.

That split could not be healed by God alone since He is not a man. No man could heal that split because he is not God. Only a being who is both God and man could bring together the gap between Heaven and earth. It is only Yeshua who is both God and man (see Rom. 1:3-4). Therefore, it is in Him that everything, whether in Heaven or in earth, will come back together into one.

Ephesians 1:10
That in the dispensation of the fullness of the times He might gather together in one all things in Christ, both which are in heaven and which are on earth—in Him.

This is why we preach the gospel in Yeshua's name. He has all authority both in Heaven and in earth.

Matthew 28:18
All authority has been given to me in heaven and on earth.

Yeshua is the central figure of the Bible, because He is the primary agent of God's plan. It is through Him that God offers us forgiveness; through Him that God judges our sin; and through Him that God will ultimately bring about perfect harmony in Heaven and earth. He alone is the Messiah.

False Messiahs

In Yeshua's teaching on the endtimes (the Olivet discourse), His first words were to watch out for deceptive teachings.

Matthew 24:4
Take heed that no one deceives you.

Four times in Matthew 24 He warns us about deception. It is important that we keep the second coming of Yeshua as the center of our teaching on the endtimes. If we get diverted from that focus, we may become deceived. Yeshua particularly warned about false messianic figures.

Matthew 24:5,11
For many will come in My name saying, "I am [the Messiah]*," and will deceive many.*

Then many false prophets will rise up and deceive many.

Mark 13:22
For false [messiahs] *and false prophets will rise and show signs and wonders to deceive, if possible, even the elect.*

In Israel we have seen many false messiahs. Rabbi Schneerson of the Lubavitch movement was touted by his followers to be the Messiah. When he became sick, his followers quoted Isaiah 53, saying he was bearing the sicknesses of the Jewish people. When he died in 1994, many of his followers expected him to rise from the dead. He didn't. But even today, one finds huge posters all over the country with Rabbi Schneerson's picture, proclaiming, "Blessed is he who comes, King Messiah."

Another large cult in Israel is the Breslav movement. Their head rabbi, Nahmun of Breslav, died in Poland almost two hundred years ago. His followers believe that he sent a note from the "afterworld" to one of their members saying that if the people of Israel would repeat the following word play on his name—Na, Nah, Nahman, Meuman—then world redemption would come. To this day, stickers and graffiti are plastered all around Israel with this messianic mantra.

Sometimes when a popular political figure wins an election, his followers chant his name to the tune of "David, King of Israel." The combination of right wing political zealotry with rabbinic religious mysticism in

Israel is a dangerous trend. Some of the followers of Rabbi Aryeh Deri were using messianic terms concerning him even while he was jailed for stealing money from the government. I can remember certain Christians proclaiming Benjamin Netanyahu's "anointing" while he was being exposed in the Israeli press for committing adultery.

The new Raelian cult has become very popular in Israel at the time of this writing. Its leader, a mystic from France, claims that he was visited by aliens from another planet. He further claims that these aliens are the God/gods, "Elohim" of the Bible. They claim that the creation of Adam was done by cloning of these aliens. Therefore they are doing experiments to clone human beings. Through this cloning they see themselves as creating life and therefore becoming gods. Rael himself proclaims forthrightly that he is the Messiah and plans to come to Jerusalem to build a new temple. Israel is central to the messianic aspirations of the Raelians.

Not Focused on the Antichrist

One of the first questions asked about the endtimes is, "Who will be the antichrist?" There have been theories about Henry Kissinger or Yassar Arafat or the Pope or the leader of the trilateral commission. While there are valid questions concerning the coming of the antichrist figure, getting more focused on the antichrist than upon Yeshua is already going in the wrong direction.

Other people ask about the time schedule of the endtimes. That is also a diversion. The question is not, when He is returning, but what we will be doing when He comes (see Acts 1:7; Lk. 12:43; 18:8; 2 Pet. 3:11).

Some people are looking primarily to the Rapture. But the focus is not on our going out, but on His coming back. The blessed hope is not the Rapture but the Second Coming (see Tit. 2:13).

One negative effect of the "antichrist" focus is that it produces more fear than faith. Our view of the endtimes is to be a victorious one. The end of the story is that the good guys win. Yeshua is coming back to conquer and to establish His kingdom upon the earth. We need to go forward with establishing the kingdom, instead of looking for ways to hide.

A Victorious Eschatology

Yeshua is infinitely stronger than satan and the antichrist together. In fact, after it is all over, people will be shocked to see both the antichrist and satan, because they will seem so weak (see Is. 14:16).

The only power that satan has in this world is through his deception of human beings and their unwitting cooperation with him. The message of the Book of Revelation is a victorious one, in which the forces of light conquer the forces of darkness.

Revelation 11:15b
The kingdoms of this world have become the kingdoms of our Lord and of His [Messiah], and He shall reign forever and ever!

Yeshua is coming in victory, and we who share our faith with Him also share in that victory.

Revelation 12:11
And they overcame him [the devil] by the blood of the Lamb and by the word of their testimony, and they did not love their lives to the death.

To all seven churches in the Book of Revelation, Yeshua sends a message challenging them to be overcomers. We are representatives of the conquering King in this world. We are spiritual soldiers of the army that wins the war.

Many people are concerned about the "mark of the beast" (see Rev. 13). However, we have something stronger than the mark of the beast—the "seal" of the Holy Spirit.

Revelation 7:3
Do not harm the earth, the sea or the trees till we have sealed the servants of God on their foreheads.

Our "mark" will be stronger than the unbelievers' "mark." Even during the time of tribulation and persecution, the saints of God will have special protection by angelic forces. As the children of Israel in Goshen were protected during the plagues of Egypt (see Ex. 9:23; 10:23), so will the people of God be protected in the plagues of the endtimes. As Peter was rescued from Herod's prison by angels (see Acts 12), so will we have angelic protection if we are fervent in prayer. As Yeshua slipped through the hands of those who were trying to kill Him (see Lk. 4:29; Jn. 7:30; 8:59; 10:39) because "His time had not yet come," so can we be protected until our time comes.

Psalm 91:7,10-11
A thousand may fall at your side and ten thousand at your right hand; but it shall not come near you.

No evil shall befall you, nor shall any plague come near your dwelling;

For He shall give His angels charge over you, to keep you in all your ways.

The supernatural protection that is described here is an important promise for us both now and in the endtimes. Psalm 91 should become a daily confession of our faith.

Double Harvest

Once I jokingly said to someone, "I don't know when the Rapture is, but if it is before the Tribulation, I'm not going." There is a half-truth in this. The period of the endtimes is also the period of the greatest evangelistic harvest in the history of the world. Wherever there is great advancement in the kingdom, there is also great persecution. Our eyes should not be focused on the tribulation, but on the harvest.

There are two great harvests in the endtimes: One good, one bad.

Revelation 14:15b-16

The time has come for You to reap, for the harvest of the earth is ripe.

So He who sat on the cloud thrust in His sickle on the earth, and the earth was reaped.

This is the first harvest. It is a good harvest. It is a time where millions of people will be saved. It should be the greatest desire of our hearts to be involved in this great harvest.

Revelation 14:17,19

Then another angel came out of the temple which is in heaven, he also having a sharp sickle.

So the angel thrust his sickle into the earth and gathered the vine of the earth, and threw it into the great winepress of the wrath of God.

This is a second harvest. It comes from "another" angel. It has a different goal. The first harvest is to save those who are willing to believe. The second harvest is to punish those who are evil. These two harvests reflect the grace and the judgment of God. They both take place in the endtimes. They both give glory to God.

The Great Commission

Our focus is not the persecution, but the harvest. It is not the "Great Tribulation" but the "Great Commission." Our job in the endtimes is to continue to preach the Kingdom of God right up until the end (see Mt. 24:14).

When people are involved in supernatural gifts and spiritual warfare without evangelism, they can fall into a kind of mysticism that easily leads to deception. When Paul taught on spiritual warfare, his closing statement was to pray for the gospel to be proclaimed with boldness (see Eph. 6:20). Prophetic ministry that is not connected to ongoing evangelism will often become imbalanced.

The same is true for pastoral and apostolic ministries. There is a degree of conflict and confrontation when we present the gospel to an unsaved and antagonistic world. When pastors and apostles are not involved in evangelism, that measure of conflict and confrontation becomes focused too much within the body of believers. Lack of emphasis on evangelism causes division and competition among believers.

This is true everywhere, and Israel is no exception. Because this is the "Holy Land," many groups are drawn to establish their ministries here. However, because of the difficulty of sharing the gospel, many of these ministries get diverted to a secondary agenda. This might be the only place in the world where there are more ministers than there are believers.

Before people are deceived, they are first diverted. The issue is not the timing of the Rapture, nor the identity of the antichrist, nor the mark of the beast. It is not the ashes of the red heifer, nor a foundation stone for the third temple, nor a plot to blow up the Dome of the Rock. One of the best ways to keep from being deceived is to concentrate on the central figure—Yeshua; on our primary task—evangelism; and on the main event—the Second Coming.

CHAPTER 4

THE HEBREW PROPHETS

The culminating event of human history is the coming of the Messiah in glory—the second coming of Yeshua. He came the first time to be crucified; the second time He will come to be glorified. He came the first time as a suffering servant; the second time He will come as a conquering King.

The Robe Dipped in Blood

Let us look again at the New Testament portrait of the Second Coming:

Revelation 19:11,13-15

Now I saw heaven opened, and behold, a white horse. And He who sat on him was called Faithful and True, and in righteousness He judges and makes war.

He was clothed with a robe dipped in blood, and His name is called The Word of God.

And the armies in heaven, clothed in fine linen, white and clean, followed Him on white horses.

Now out of His mouth goes a sharp sword, that with it He should strike the nations. And He Himself will rule them with a rod of iron. He Himself treads the winepress of the fierceness and wrath of Almighty God.

Recently I was asked whether the phrase "robe dipped in blood" referred to His own blood at the Crucifixion, or the blood of those slain at the Second Coming. My answer was that it refers to both, but that in the context of Revelation 19, it refers primarily to the blood of those slain by Him.

One of the keys to understanding Revelation 19 is to realize that John is quoting from Isaiah.

Isaiah 63:2-4a

Why is your apparel red, and your garments like one who treads in the winepress?

I have trodden the winepress alone, and from the peoples no one was with Me. For I have trodden them in My anger, and trampled them in My fury; their blood is sprinkled upon My garments, and I have stained all My robes.

For the day of vengeance is in My heart.

Both the image of the garment being stained with blood and the image of trampling out the winepress of wrath quoted in Revelation 19 are taken from Isaiah 63. In fact there are many parallels in the last chapters of Isaiah with the last chapters of Revelation.

The Stars Will Fall

Isaiah speaks of the heavens being torn open (see Is. 64:1) as John speaks of the heavens being opened (see Rev. 19:11). Isaiah also speaks of fire going forth before the Lord (see Is. 64:2) and of the new heavens and new earth (see Is. 65:17; 66:22), which are New Testament themes. John speaks of the glory of New Jerusalem (see Rev. 21), which is a theme repeated throughout Isaiah. (See chapters 24, 25, 35, 43, 51, 52, 54, 60–61.)

New Testament prophecies about the endtimes are quoting and expanding the prophecies of the Tenach (Old Testament). The Hebrew prophets provide the context for the New Testament apocalypse. One reason there has been so much confusion concerning New Testament eschatology is that it is taken out of that context. To gain a better view, we should interpret New Testament eschatology within its context of the Hebrew prophets.

Another example is found in Revelation 6:13-14, which states that the stars will fall to the ground, the sky will recede and be rolled up like a scroll, and the mountains will be removed out of their places. Here John is quoting and expanding upon Isaiah 34:3b-4a "The mountains shall be melted with their blood. All the host of heaven shall be dissolved, and the heavens shall be rolled up like a scroll." The context of this quote is the vengeance of Zion in battle against Edom and all the nations of the world.

The Context of the Olivet Discourse

The New Testament gives a revelation of the angelic warfare that takes place during the great end-times war in which the nations of the world come against Israel to battle. Unless we see the angelic warfare of the New Testament apocalypse in its context of the end-times war against Israel, those heavenly battles become incomprehensible.

Perhaps the best example is Yeshua's own teaching on the Second Coming.

Matthew 24:29-31
Immediately after the tribulation of those days the sun will be darkened, and the moon will not give its light; the stars will fall from heaven, and the powers of the heavens will be shaken.

Then the sign of the Son of Man will appear in heaven, and then all the tribes of the earth will mourn, and they will see the Son of Man coming on the clouds of heaven with power and great glory.

And He will send His angels with a great sound of a trumpet, and they will gather together His elect from the four winds, from one end of heaven to the other.

Some people picture Yeshua here like a guru on the Mount of Olives with His disciples sitting before Him. They ask Him a question about the endtimes. He goes into a sort of trance and pronounces these mystical prophecies that no one could possibly understand.

But that is not what is happening. Yeshua is a Bible teacher. His Bible is the Hebrew Tenach. His disciples ask Him a question, and He explains to them from the texts of the prophets that refer to the subject.

In Matthew 24:29 Yeshua speaks of the "tribulation." Here He is referring to Jeremiah 30:7b, "It is the time of Jacob's trouble, but he shall be saved out of it." The phrase here for "time of trouble" in the Hebrew is *eit tsara*, from which we derive the New Testament concept of "tribulation." It is also found in Daniel 12:1b, "And there shall be a time of trouble, such as never was since there was a nation, even to that time. And at that time your people shall be delivered, every one who is found written in the book."

In both of the passages that Yeshua is quoting, the prophecies state that Israel will be saved. It is during the very period of the end-times Tribulation that salvation will come to Israel. Yes, there will be tribulation in the endtime. That tribulation leads up to a giant war, at which point Yeshua will return. But it is also during that period of tribulation that the gospel will bear the most fruit in Israel and around the world.

How Will Israel Be Saved?

At the end of the Tribulation, right before Yeshua comes back, this great promise will be fulfilled:

Romans 11:26a
And so all Israel will be saved.

This verse is one of the guiding motivations for our ministry in Israel. While we often encounter opposition, we know that we are "doomed to succeed." I am often asked how I see this promised revival coming about in Israel. I see it coming in several stages, from small to large. The Bible speaks of three basic levels:

1. *A few*—At first there is a great effort at evangelism, even though a relatively small number come to the Lord. Paul said that one of the effects of the gospel bearing fruit among the Gentiles is that it might attract Jewish people and "save some of them" (see Rom. 11:17). He said of himself, as a Messianic Jew, that he would do everything to conform himself culturally to the customs of our people in order to "by all means save some" (see 1 Cor. 9:20-22). This is the period we are in now.

2. *Many*—The Bible then states that during the endtimes tribulation, many Israelis will come to the Lord. That is the period yet before us. Revelation 7:4b refers to the number of Israelis coming to the Lord during the Tribulation as "One hundred and forty-four thousand [144,000] of all the tribes of the children of Israel were sealed."

3. *All*—Toward the end of the Tribulation, right before the second coming of Yeshua, revival will spread to the whole nation, so that, "all Israel will be saved." That final revival, affecting the entire nation, may come at the end of such terrible wars and tribulations, that two-thirds of the nation will be killed. Then the entire remnant of the one-third who survive will turn to the Lord (see Zech. 13:9).

These three general stages (some—many—all) are connected one to another. There will not be a national revival preceding the Second Coming unless there is a remnant saved and sharing their faith during the Tribulation. And there will not be a tribulation remnant if we are not "doing all to save some" during the present time.

Zechariah chapters 12, 13, and 14 speak of the same idea of salvation during tribulation, concerning Jerusalem. As we look at the first few verses of each of those chapters, we see an interesting pattern.

Zechariah 12: Jerusalem becomes a point of international controversy.

Zechariah 13: A spiritual fountain of forgiveness and cleansing is opened to the inhabitants of Jerusalem.

Zechariah 14: The nations of the world attack Jerusalem at the second coming of Yeshua.

It doesn't take a prophet to recognize that Jerusalem has already become the most controversial political issue in the international arena. The fountain of revival is just beginning.

During the midst of the Zechariah sequence we find that beautiful passage, "And I will pour out on the house of David and on the inhabitants of Jerusalem the Spirit of grace and supplication; then they will look on Me whom they pierced" (see Zech. 12:10). The word for "on" in this verse may be mistranslated. To look "on Me" would be *alay*, while in this case it is *eilay*, which is better translated as look "to Me." There is a dual meaning here prophetically, both to see Yeshua when He returns, and to turn *toward* Him as Savior in the period before He returns.

Some people use this verse to say that there is no need to share the gospel in Israel. They think that the people will be saved supernaturally without the gospel at the moment of the Second Coming when they look "upon" Yeshua. That is not true. We are to share the gospel now, so that as many as possible will look "toward" or "to" Yeshua and be saved. Even those who will look "upon" Him at the Second Coming will need to have heard about Him through the preaching of the gospel prior to that time.

Second Pentecost

In Matthew 24, Yeshua went on to say that the sun and the stars would be darkened and the powers of Heaven be shaken. Here He is quoting again from the Hebrew prophets.

Joel 2:30-32

And I will show wonders in the heavens and in the earth: blood and fire and pillars of smoke.

The sun shall be turned into darkness, and the moon into blood, before the coming of the great and awesome day of the Lord.

And it shall come to pass that whoever calls on the name of the Lord shall be saved. For in Mount Zion and in Jerusalem there shall be deliverance, as the Lord has said, among the remnant whom the Lord calls.

This a logical passage for Yeshua to teach about, because it describes what takes place immediately before "the coming of the great and awesome day of the Lord." How different Yeshua's teaching now looks when we see it in the context of what He was quoting from Joel 2. These verses speak of the Messianic remnant in Israel, world revival, tribulation, and eventually the Lord's returning to bring restoration to the nation of Israel and peace to the world.

This passage from Joel is also the passage that Peter quoted at Pentecost, referring to the revival and outpouring of the Holy Spirit in Jerusalem.

Joel 2:28-29

And it shall come to pass afterward that I will pour out My Spirit on all flesh; your sons and daughters shall prophesy...

I will pour out My Spirit in those days.

Both Yeshua and Peter are saying that in the end-times tribulation right before the Second Coming, there will be a mighty revival in Israel, just as it was on the Day of Pentecost, but much, much bigger. Yeshua's teaching on the end-times in Matthew 24 quotes Joel 2, which says that God will pour out His Spirit upon Israel. Peter's preaching in Acts 2 quotes Joel 2 about the outpouring of the Holy Spirit that will take place in the end-times.

The events of Acts 2 were not the final fulfillment of Joel's prophecy of revival. They could not have been, because Joel's prophecy deals with the period of tribulation right before the Second Coming. Yeshua confirmed that viewpoint by teaching on Joel 2 concerning the end-times.

Yeshua quoted Joel 2 concerning the end-times. Peter quoted Joel 2 concerning revival. If we put the two together, we see that they both refer to a great revival that will take place in the endtimes. The events of Acts 2 began a revival that for the past two thousand years has been spreading slowly around the world through evangelism. That evangelism will result in a great harvest of souls all over the world and will culminate in a mighty revival in Israel.

The Hebrew Prophets and the Olivet Discourse

In Matthew 24:30, Yeshua says that all the tribes of the earth will mourn. Here He is quoting from Zechariah 12:10-14. Looking at these passages in the context of the Hebrew prophets, we clearly see the connection to revival in Israel and the coming attack of the nations of the world against Jerusalem.

Yeshua then says that people will see "the Son of Man coming on the clouds of heaven" (Mt. 24:30). Here He is quoting from Daniel 7:13b, which says "And behold, One like the Son of Man, coming with the clouds of heaven." This is part of Daniel's prophecy concerning the coming of the Messiah, who would establish His kingdom on earth over the all peoples and nations.

Finally, Yeshua refers to His angels gathering His elect from the four winds of heaven at the great sound of the trumpet (see Mt. 24:31). Again Yeshua is quoting from the Hebrew prophets:

Isaiah 27:12b-13

And you will be gathered one by one, O you children of Israel.

So it shall be in that day: The great trumpet will be blown; they will come, who are about to perish in the land of Assyria, and they who are outcasts in the land of Egypt, and shall worship the Lord in the holy mount at Jerusalem.

The reference to the Rapture in Matthew 24:31 is part of Isaiah's prophecy concerning the regathering of the nation of Israel. The Matthew passage only states that the elect will be gathered from the four corners of the earth. He says *from where* they are gathered, but not *to where* they will be gathered.

Most people assume Yeshua meant that they will be gathered into heavenly Jerusalem in the sky. However, in context, the elect are being gathered to come worship Him at the holy mount in physical Israel. Yeshua added several elements not found in the Isaiah passage, such as the involvement of the angels and the gathering of all the elect, not just the children of Israel. He did not mention the children of Israel and the gathering to Jerusalem, because that would have been obvious and understood by His disciples who knew the prophecies of Isaiah.

In summary, when Yeshua taught about His second coming in Matthew 24:29-31, He was teaching from the Bible and explaining prophecies from Jeremiah 30, Daniel 7 and 12, Zechariah 12, Joel 2, and Isaiah 27. Yeshua always taught from the Old Testament (Tenach). When we understand His teaching on His second coming in the context of the Hebrew prophets, we see how it is connected to revival in Israel and the establishment of the Messianic kingdom on earth.

The Three Parts of the Kingdom

Now we can better understand the reaction of Yeshua's disciples to His teachings about the Kingdom of God in Acts 1. From Yeshua's teachings from the Hebrew prophets, they understood that the Kingdom of God was connected to the restoration of Israel.

Acts 1:6
Therefore, when they had come together, they asked Him, saying,
"Lord, will You at this time restore the kingdom to Israel?"

Yeshua responded that two other elements had to be included before the restoration of the kingdom: The receiving of the Holy Spirit and world evangelism.

Acts 1:8
But you shall receive power when the Holy Spirit has come upon
you; and you shall be witnesses to Me in Jerusalem, and in all
Judea and Samaria, and to the end of the earth.

The Kingdom of God is made up of three complementary parts. The first is the Holy Spirit's living inside of human beings. If the disciples had gone forth to establish the kingdom in Israel before the outpouring of the Holy Spirit, God could have dwelt in their midst through the cloud in the temple. However, God's plan and desire for the human race have always been for Him to live inside of us through the Holy Spirit. Therefore, Yeshua told His disciples that the kingdom could not be established without the integral part of the indwelling of the Holy Spirit.

Secondly, God's plan was for all types of human beings to enjoy loving fellowship with God and with one another. That kind of unity cannot happen until all human beings are presented the gospel, through which we are given fellowship with God and reconciliation with one another. In the international community of faith, we are supposed to be a network of people, like a rainbow, in relationships of love and harmony.

Finally, God's plan is for a perfect society to be established on earth, with Yeshua as the reigning monarch and with Jerusalem as its capital. It will be a real society, with real people and real activity. There will be peace and prosperity on earth. It will be like the kingdom of David and Solomon at its best, only better, larger, and eternal. Instead of David or Solomon, Yeshua will be the King.

So, if you can envision a perfect society on earth, like an enlarged Davidic kingdom; a perfect international community of faith with unity in diversity; and the fullness of God dwelling in the human race, you can get a good idea of what the Kingdom of God will be like. In the meantime, we have these goals before us: The infilling of the Holy Spirit, world evangelism, and the restoration of Israel. That is our passion.

CHAPTER 5

PEACE IN THE MIDDLE EAST

Peace. Shalom. Saalam. Everyone wants peace. Is it possible? Will there ever be peace in the Middle East? Actually, yes. Peace in the Middle East, extending all over the world, is a central aspect of the Kingdom of God. It is the dream of all the Hebrew prophets.

Vision for Peace

The New Age movement has a slogan: *Visualize World Peace.* I agree with that. We are to visualize world peace. The question is what kind of peace? How can we achieve it? And who determines what that peaceful world will look like?

Isaiah 2:1-4
The word that Isaiah the son of Amoz saw concerning Judah and Jerusalem…

Now it shall come to pass in the latter days that the mountain of the Lord's house shall be established on the top of the mountains, and shall be exalted above the hills; and all nations shall flow to it.

…For out of Zion shall go forth the law, and the word of the Lord from Jerusalem.

He shall judge between the nations, and rebuke many people; they shall beat their swords into plowshares, and their spears into pruning hooks; nation shall not lift up sword against nation, neither shall they learn war anymore.

Here we have the biblical vision of peace on earth. There are other visions and plans for peace, but they are false. If we want real peace, we must cooperate with God's plan. Other efforts to make peace may be well-intentioned, but if they do not go along with God's peace, they will not produce results; they may even be counterproductive.

Jeremiah 6:14

They have also healed the hurt of My people slightly, saying, "Peace, peace!" when there is no peace."

When does God's peace take place? "In the latter days." The final stage of the kingdom will take place at the end of the age. We are on a road that will end up in peace, but that total peace does not come until the end. Since God is for peace, we are for peace—peace at any time. Since we want real peace, we often have to oppose seemingly peaceful solutions that do not deal with the root of the problem.

The laws of the Torah (see Deut. 20) teach that we should first pursue peace, but if that peace is not accepted, we must deal with the situation militarily. David said:

Psalm 120:6-7

My soul has dwelt too long with one who hates peace.

I am for peace; but when I speak, they are for war.

We are for peace—even partial peace. But we must not be deceived to think that lasting peace will take place until all the elements of Isaiah's vision are in place. Even though David was for peace, he had to fight many wars. He dealt with the reality that those around him were for war. In our hearts we are "peaceniks," but the reality often forces us to be more "security" oriented. We have an olive branch in one hand and the sword in the other.

And where will God's peace take place? In "Zion," or Jerusalem. Jerusalem is seen as the international capital of this world peace. The vision of peace is actually a vision "concerning Jerusalem."

And who will be part of it? "All nations," "many peoples." The international Messianic peace will include every nation of the world. It is not for one ethnic group, but for all. It is a multiracial vision. We reject all racism as totally against the principles of the Bible.

This vision of world peace is repeated by many of the prophets. (See Isaiah 35, 60–66; Jeremiah 33; Ezekiel 40–48; Joel 3; Zechariah 14; and Micah 4.) The prophecy in Micah 4 repeats word for word Isaiah's vision, but adds another phrase, "Everyone shall sit under his vine and under his fig tree" (Mic. 4:4a)." This phrase is a biblical symbol for economic prosperity. The Messianic age includes not only peace, but also prosperity.

Which Comes First?

Isaiah's words "beating swords into plowshares" means that weapons of war will be converted into agricultural tools, that is, for peaceful use. This action could be interpreted in one of two possibilities: Disarmament at a peace agreement or the conversion of weapons at the conclusion of a war.

Unfortunately, the biblical view is the latter. In the prophet Joel, the Messianic peace follows directly after the war of the "valley of Jehoshaphat" (Joel 3:2). In Zechariah, it follows the battle in which all nations will be gathered against Jerusalem (see Zech. 14:2). In Ezekiel, it follows the war of "Gog and Magog":

Ezekiel 39:9

Those who dwell in the cities of Israel will go out and set on fire and burn the weapons, both the shields...and spears; and they will make fires with them for seven years.

This is Ezekiel's description of the swords being beaten into plowshares. It obviously takes place immediately after the apocalyptic war. The victors in the war will take the enemy's armaments and use them for civilian energy needs. Then they will take their own weapons (swords) and turn them to civilian use (plowshares) as well.

So there will be a time of peaceful disarmament and prosperity in the Middle East before the great war. It is the very prosperity of Israel and the lowering of its defense forces that attracts the nations of the world to attack. A major event is coming in the Middle East that will bring a period of peace and disarmament. Israel will experience an enormous economic boom. The nations will become jealous and, noticing Israel's lack of defenses, will mount a final attack of huge proportions.

Ezekiel 38:11-12

You will say, "I will go up against a land of unwalled villages; I will go to a peaceful people, who dwell safely, all of them dwelling without walls, and neither having bars nor gates"—

To take plunder and to take booty...of livestock and goods...

The phrase, "unwalled villages" in Hebrew is perazot, from which we derive the modern Hebrew word for "disarmament." The current crisis in the Middle East will eventually lead to a peace accord, with disarmament and economic prosperity for Israel; which will lead to a united international military attack upon Israel; which will lead to the coming of the Messiah and the era of true world peace.

The Prince of Peace

Isaiah's vision in chapter 2 of the Book of Isaiah continues in chapter 9, where the emphasis is not so much on the place from whence the peace will flow, but on the person who will bring it about.

Isaiah 9:6-7a

For unto us a Child is born, unto us a Son is given; and the government will be upon His shoulder. And His name will be called Wonderful, Counselor, Mighty God, Everlasting Father, Prince of Peace.

Of the increase of His government and peace there will be no end, upon the throne of David and over his kingdom, to order it and establish it with judgment and justice.

If God is going to bring peace to a real world, He has to start with some real place and with some real person. The first person whom God found was Abraham. He cut a covenant with him—a kind of peace treaty between God and man. Then He sent him to the Promised Land to start a family, a tribe, and a nation. (Abraham is considered the father of faith to Jews, Christians, and Muslims alike.)

Abraham brought the first hope for peace. In the covenant that Abraham cut, God promised that one of Abraham's offspring would bring about the ultimate peace for all nations (see Gen. 22:18).

The hope for world peace continued through the nation that came from Abraham until it developed into the kingdom of David. David's kingdom accomplished part of the vision for world peace, but not all of it. God continued His promise to David that one of his offspring would bring the eternal peaceful kingdom (see 2 Sam. 7:14).

That promised offspring of Abraham and David is the Messiah. He is the instrument of world peace. He is the Prince of Peace. That person is Yeshua. He came to sit "upon the throne of David and over his kingdom" (Is. 9:7). This is what the angel Gabriel told Miriam (Mary) about the child that would be born through her:

Luke 1:32-33

He will be great, and will be called the Son of the Highest; and the Lord God will give Him the throne of His father David.

And He will reign over the house of Jacob forever, and of His kingdom there will be no end.

When Yeshua was born, the shepherds heard the angels cry:

Luke 2:14
Glory to God in the highest, and on earth peace, good will toward men.

Yeshua came to fulfill the prophecy of Isaiah 9—to be the Prince of Peace and to sit upon the throne of David. He expanded the covenant of Abraham into a new and fuller covenant. He extended the kingdom of David into eternity.

Perfect peace on earth cannot be brought about by a normal king. It is a job for a supernatural figure. Isaiah describes Him as "Immanuel" (God with us)" and "mighty God, everlasting Father" (Is. 7:14; 9:6). The peace He will bring is so supernatural that even the "wolf also shall dwell with the lamb...the nursing child shall play by the cobra's hole" (Is. 11:6-8). That kind of peace can be brought about only by Yeshua.

Root of Rebellion

Why is there such conflict in the world, and particularly in the Middle East? Why is there so much hatred and corruption? According to the Bible, the problems in the world are caused by the fact that mankind in general is in rebellion against God.

It is God's will to bring peace and prosperity. However, the root of sin and rebellion must be driven out before there can be lasting peace and prosperity. The heart of man is described as deceitful, selfish and even "desperately wicked" (Jer. 17:9). There can be no peace unless the heart of man is changed.

In the Middle East, no matter what political treaty is proposed or signed, it will do no good as long as Jews and Arabs hate one another. The roots of their enmity go back 35 hundred years. The same is true for any two people groups. Take away a man's weapons, and he can strike his neighbor with a stick. Take away the stick, he can strike him with his fist.

There was peace and prosperity in the Garden of Eden before the sin of man. There will be peace and prosperity in the restoration of the earth in the age to come, but it can happen only when sin has been rooted out of the heart of man and the forces of rebellion in the world have been destroyed.

Psalm 2:1-3
Why do the nations rage, and the people plot a vain thing?

The kings of the earth set themselves, and the rulers take counsel together, against the Lord and against His Anointed, saying,

"Let us break their bonds in pieces and cast away their cords from us."

The world is in rebellion not only against God, but also against "His anointed," that is, the *Mashiach*, (Messiah). The authority of God from Heaven is expressed through the person of the Messiah. Therefore the rebellion against God takes the form of rebellion against the Messiah. He who rejects God's Messiah has in effect rebelled against God's authority.

The Person and the Place

The Messiah is also referred to as "My King" in Psalm 2:6. The Messiah is God's king upon the earth. This Messiah king is also referred to as God's Son (see Ps. 2:7.12). (The idea that the Messiah would be God's Son is not a New Testament invention, but rather a viewpoint rooted in the Hebrew prophets. The Jewish world sees the Messiah as a king, but misses him as God's Son. The Christian world sees Yeshua as God's Son, but misses him as the king of Israel.)

Psalm 2:6-7

Yet I have set My King on My holy hill of Zion...

The Lord has said to Me, "You are My Son, today I have begotten You."

So God has established His authority on earth through a certain person—Yeshua. But He has also chosen a certain place—Jerusalem. He has set His king upon His hill. The hill as well as the king is an expression of God's authority on the earth. We, the human race, have to accept God's chosen person and His chosen place.

These two expressions of God's authority—His person and His place—constitute a test for mankind. It is a test of heart to see whether we will submit to the will of God. It is through God's chosen person and His chosen place that God detects the root of sin and rebellion in man.

Many Christians accept the person, but not the place. Many Jews accept the place, but not the person. Much of the world rejects both. We accept both Jesus and Jerusalem.

The current war in the Middle East is called the "Al Aqsa" intifada, or the "Dome of the Rock" uprising. That very spot is called the "mountain of the Lord" in Isaiah 2:3, and "My holy hill" in Psalm 2:6. The phrase in Hebrew is *Har HaBayit*, which is also translated as "the Temple Mount." It is the focal point of conflict because God chose it as a reference point of His authority (see Zech. 12:2-3). The Bible calls that place "Zion"; the Islamic world calls it "Al Aqsa."

The Double Judgment

The struggle as to whether the human race will submit to God's authority will find its inevitable outcome in the great apocalyptic war, which immediately precedes the coming of the Messiah. This war will be started by the ungodly nations of the world and will be stopped by Yeshua Himself.

Zechariah 14:2-4a

I will gather all the nations to battle against Jerusalem....

Then the Lord will go forth and fight against those nations, as He fights in the day of battle.

And in that day His feet will stand on the Mount of Olives.

The "feet on the Mount of Olives" are the feet of Yeshua as He returns to earth. The battle mentioned here takes place over God's chosen place and is won by God's chosen person.

Yeshua considers the attack upon Jerusalem as an attack upon Himself. The nations of the world who attack Jerusalem may not realize that they are attacking the Messiah, but God sees it that way. This conflict is the final test of submission to God's authority. It is at this point that Yeshua returns to sit on David's throne.

At the Second Coming, not only will the nations who attack Jerusalem be destroyed, but also every person who refuses to submit to the authority of Yeshua will be judged.

2 Thessalonians 1:7b-8

When the Lord Jesus is revealed from Heaven with His mighty angels,

In flaming fire taking vengeance on those who do not know God, and on those who do not obey the gospel of our Lord Jesus [the Messiah].

The nations will be judged as to whether they attacked Jerusalem. Individual persons will be judged as to whether they obeyed the message of Yeshua. The governments of this world must respect God's authority in His chosen capital. Every person must accept God's authority in His chosen king.

Fighting Against God

On that day of double judgment, I do not want to be found fighting against God. How do we know whether God is on our side? Perhaps He is on our opponent's side. God forbid! It is our duty to search the Scriptures to make sure we are in line with God's will.

It is not impossible to know the will of God. Sincere repentance and scripture meditation can bring us the answer. God wants us to know His will. Could we deceive ourselves? Of course, it is possible. That is why honesty and humility are so essential.

The question is not whether God is on our side, but whether we are on His side. As we saw in the encounter with the divine Messenger before the battle of Jericho, Joshua asked, "Are you for us or for our adversaries?" The Man did not say which side he was on, but rather reversed the question: "No, but as the Commander of the army of the Lord I have now come" (see Josh.5:13-14).

God is not taking sides. He is not for Jew or Christian, Israeli or Arab, secular or religious. He has set the standard. It is up to us to align ourselves with Him. He already has a side—His own. Let's find out which side He is on and get on it. When Yeshua comes back, will we be found fighting for Him or against Him?

He will come. And He will fight. There is no doubt about that. He will fight against those who disobey the gospel (see 2 Thess. 1:8), against the nations that have attacked Jerusalem (see Zech. 14:2), and against those who are in rebellion to God's authority (see Ps. 2:9).

All human beings need to submit themselves to God. There is no one who does not need to repent. We have all sinned and fallen short of God's standard (see Rom. 3:23). All of us by our own human nature have been rebels and enemies to God at one time (see Eph. 2:2-3).

Every person must submit his life to Yeshua. It does not matter what his background is or whether he seems to be a relatively good person. Even the most Torah-observant, ultra-orthodox Jewish rabbi in the world needs to undergo a radical change of heart and be "born again" (see Jn. 3:3).

The world will have to recognize God's covenant claim to Jerusalem. Any nation that attacks Jerusalem in that final day will be destroyed. It does not matter whether that nation calls itself Christian or Muslim. It does matter whether they have a mandate from the United Nations or the European Common Market.

The nations of the world face one question, which overrides other political and military concerns—whether or not they will be part of that united attack against Jerusalem. The question is not whether the United States destroys the forces of bin Laden in Afghanistan or Saddam Hussein in Iraq. The crucial point is whether the public opinion, in the wake of these conflicts, will turn against Israel.

Evangelical Christians, wherever they live, should pray that their particular country, stand with Israel in the endtimes. Unfortunately, many born-again Christians do not think the passage in Zechariah 14 applies to them. However, it is Yeshua Himself who will be leading the attack on the nations who have come against Israel.

When God said that He would gather all nations against Jerusalem, He did not mean that He wants the nations to attack. He will gather the nations that are in rebellion against Him for one final showdown, where He will display His power by annihilating them. The prophecies of the judgment are to help us repent. Let us learn from the double judgment of God, and make sure we are on God's side in that day of battle.

What's the Solution?

Behind the political conflict in the Middle East is a religious one. Behind the religious conflict is a spiritual one. The true solution to the problem is to deal with the spiritual root, not the political one, nor even the religious one.

When the disciples asked Yeshua if He would restore the kingdom to Israel (see Acts 1:6), they had in mind the vision of Isaiah 2. They wanted to know if Yeshua would, at that time, bring the Messianic era. Yeshua told them that it was not yet the time (Acts 1:8).

His disciples would first have to receive the Holy Spirit and preach the gospel around the world. Then He would return to bring world peace (see Mt. 24:14). Yeshua was saying, "Yes, I will bring peace upon the earth, but first we must get rid of the spiritual root of sin and rebellion."

When everyone has had a chance to hear God's offer of peace or judgment, then Yeshua will return. The drama began in Jerusalem and will end in Jerusalem. There Yeshua was crucified as the suffering servant, and there He will return as a conquering king.

Luke 19:41-42

Now as He [Yeshua] *drew near, He saw the city* [Yerushalayim] *and wept over it,*

Saying, "If you had known, even you, especially in this your day, the things that make for your peace! But now they are hidden from your eyes."

The only one who can bring peace to the Middle East is Yeshua, the Prince of Peace. It has to be the real Yeshua of the Bible. It is not Muhammad, nor the pope, nor the chief rabbi of Israel. It is not the president of the United States, nor the secretary general of the United Nations, nor the prime minister of Israel. It is not the Catholic, Protestant or Pentecostal church. It is Yeshua Himself, both Son of God and son of David (see Rom. 1:3-4).

If only the world could know…He is the one who makes for peace.

CHAPTER 6

THE SEED OF ABRAHAM

God created Adam in His own image and gave him authority over everything on planet Earth (see Gen. 1:26-27). God also made, in His image, a group of heavenly beings we call angels. Angels and men look similar to one another because they were both made in God's image (see Heb. 13:2). In fact, both men and angels were made after the pattern of Yeshua, as He is the perfect image of God. Both men and angels are called "sons" of God, while only Yeshua is the Son of God.

There were three top "commander" angels under the authority of Yeshua and God. Their names were Michael, Gabriel, and lucifer. The name lucifer in Hebrew is *Hillel ben Shachar* (see Is. 14:12). Everything God made was good. All the angels were good, including lucifer. However, lucifer became jealous of the authority and glory given to Adam on the earth. He wanted to steal it for himself. At that moment he sinned (see Ezek. 28:15).

The temptation of Adam and Eve in the Garden of Eden was actually an attempt by lucifer to usurp Adam's authority. Lucifer's sin in the garden was greater than Adam and Eve's. It was an act of rebellion against God. He ceased to be lucifer and became satan, which means "enemy" or "accuser" in Hebrew. Since satan was commander over a third of the angels, he took them with him in the rebellion. In that way, a third of the angels became "demons," which are simply evil or rebellious angels.

Satan was not so much looking for Adam to sin, as he was looking for an opportunity to accuse Adam and bring him under his control. (According to the Bible, controlling other people through guilt manipulation is worse than sin.) Satan has sway in this world because of his influence over the sons of men. He took Adam's place as ruler over the planet. Six times in the New Testament Satan is referred to as the "god" of this world. (See Luke 4; John 12, 14, 16; Ephesians 2; Second Corinthians 4.)

The War Between the Serpent and the Woman

From the moment of the rebellion in the Garden of Eden, God declared that the day would come when He would bring one of the sons of the "woman" to destroy satan, and thereby reverse the damage that had been done.

Genesis 3:15
I will put enmity between you and the woman, and between your seed and her Seed; He shall bruise your head, and you shall bruise His heel.

This declaration of enmity against the serpent, and the promise of victory by the Seed, is the beginning of all the spiritual warfare of the Bible. From that moment on, satan looked to kill every righteous child born of woman who might be the promised seed.

Eve had two children, one good and one bad. Satan obviously thought that the good child, Abel, must be the promised seed. Therefore satan persuaded Cain with thoughts of jealousy and violence until eventually he murdered Abel. And so the story continued. Satan always tried to kill the righteous seed to prevent one of them from fulfilling the prophecy to destroy him. The symbolic picture of the giant serpent trying to kill the seed of the woman is a portrait of the spiritual warfare in every generation.

Revelation 12:1-4
Now a great sign appeared in heaven: a woman clothed with the sun, with the moon under her feet, and on her head a garland of twelve stars.

Then being with child, she cried out in labor and in pain to give birth.

And another sign appeared in heaven: behold, a great, fiery red dragon having seven heads and ten horns, and seven diadems on his heads.

His tail drew a third of the stars of heaven and threw them to the earth. And the dragon stood before the woman who was ready to give birth, to devour her Child as soon as it was born.

The persons fulfilling the role of the woman and the seed change from generation to generation, but the pattern of the spiritual warfare remains the same. Sometimes the woman was one of the matriarchs; at other times, it was the entire generation of mothers in Israel. Sometimes the seed was one of the patriarchs; at other times, it was the entire generation of male children in Israel.

Before the time of Yeshua, every Jewish mother thought she might be the one to give birth to the promised seed; and every Jewish boy was seen as a potential candidate to be the Messiah seed himself.

When Yeshua was born to Miriam, he fulfilled the promise of the coming seed. Through His death and resurrection, He delivered a mortal blow to satan and all the forces of evil.

After Yeshua went to Heaven, the battle continued with the devil trying to kill all dedicated disciples who are called to leadership in the Kingdom of God

Revelation 12:17

And the dragon was enraged with the woman, and he went to make war with the rest of her offspring, who keep the commandments of God and have the testimony of [Messiah Yeshua].

The righteous woman may be seen in different contexts as Eve, Miriam, Israel, the Church, or any godly mother. The seed may be seen as Abel, Yeshua, one of the Israeli patriarchs or prophets, or any godly young man in any generation.

The Abrahamic Covenant

Until the time of Abraham, there were no specifications to God's promise to bring the seed of the woman to destroy satan. The seed could have been the son of any woman. However, in Abraham, God found a man who was faithful and obedient. Jewish tradition says that Abraham's faith was tested ten times. The greatest test was the sacrificial love required to give his only begotten son.

Genesis 22:1-2

Now it came to pass after these things that God tested Abraham, and said to him, "Abraham!" And he said, "Here I am."

Then He said, "Take now your son, your only son Isaac, whom you love, and go to the land of Moriah, and offer him there as a burnt offering on one of the mountains of which I shall tell you."

Since faithfulness and obedience are so important in reversing the sin of Adam and the rebellion of satan, God made a covenant with Abraham that the Messianic seed would come into the world through his children. It was through Abraham's seed that the human race would be saved and blessed.

Genesis 22:18
In your seed all the nations of the earth shall be blessed, because you have obeyed My voice.

From that moment on, the spiritual battle was concentrated on this one family. The life of all human beings was dependent upon the covenant with Abraham and his descendants. They became the chosen people—not because of racial superiority—but because of faith in the coming of the Messianic seed.

Later on, the covenant of the Messianic seed would be further narrowed to Isaac, because he was willing to give his life as a sacrifice (see Gen. 22); later to Judah because he was willing to substitute his life to take the punishment for Benjamin (see Gen. 44); and finally to David after he sought to find a dwelling place for God in the earth (see 2 Sam. 7).

The Destiny of the Jewish People

The destiny of the Jewish people was wrapped up in bringing this child into the world. Satan was out to kill them in order to stop the child from being born. God had to protect them at all costs, even when they were not righteous, in order to preserve the prophesied fulfillment of the seed promise. This understanding explains many seemingly strange events of the Tenach.

For instance, God told Abimelech that He would kill him and all his people if Abimelech touched Sarah, even though it was Abraham's fault for not having told the king that they were married (see Gen. 20). Hagar and Ishmael had to be separated from Isaac even though it seemed to be cruel (see Gen. 21). Rachel said she was ready to die if she could not bear a son to Jacob (see Gen. 30). The sons of Jacob slaughtered the entire tribe of Shechem because he had slept with their sister Dinah (see Gen. 34). It was imperative that the bloodline of the covenant not be ruined through immorality.

Judah's daughter-in-law Tamar posed as a whore and became pregnant after having relations with him (see Gen. 38). Afterwards, Judah confessed that she was more righteous than he (see Gen. 38:26). God changed history around to move Ruth, a righteous Gentile, to be brought to Boaz, in order to preserve the line of the Messiah (see Ruth 4). I even believe that Bat Sheva was destined to be the mother of the Messianic line, and had David not intervened through sin, her first husband, Uriah (of the illegal Hittite tribe), would have been killed in war anyway to enable her to come to David in a righteous manner (see 2 Sam. 11).

All those events occurred to protect the continuance of the promised seed. This is also why the sign of the Abrahamic covenant was cut on the male organ (see Gen. 17) and why there were such strict laws concerning female menstrual blood or male semen emission (see Lev. 12, 15, 18). It explains why intermarriage was considered a sin more grievous than idolatry (see Ezra 9).

In the New Testament we find Zechariah the high priest in the temple praying for his wife Elisheva (Elizabeth) to bear a child (see Lk. 1:13), Simeon and Anna in the temple interceding for the birth of the baby Messiah (see Lk. 2), and Joseph, of the lineage of King David, in a moral dilemma about his fiancée, Miriam, who is pregnant out of wedlock (see Mt. 1).

Hatred Against the Seed

Not only does this perspective explain the spiritual "gymnastics" of the Jewish people to keep the Messianic seed covenant intact, it also explains the many attacks of violence against them. God and His servants were trying to keep them alive, while satan and his servants were trying to kill them. As long as the Messianic seed was within the Jewish people, they all became a target of attack. The people as a whole were the "seed of Abraham," because the seed of the Messiah was in them.

Esau wanted to kill Jacob after Jacob tricked him out of his birthright (see Gen. 27). The brothers of Joseph tried to kill him because of their jealousy (see Gen. 37). In Egypt, the children of Israel multiplied in such numbers that it was impossible to identify who the seed candidate was. Therefore a satanic attempt was made by Pharaoh to murder all of the Israelite male children (see Ex. 1). When Saul realized that David had the Messianic anointing, he also tried to kill him out of jealousy (see 1 Sam. 18-26).

All of the evil nations tried to attack and kill the people of Israel—the people of the covenant. The issue was more than racial anti-Semitism; it was a satanic spiritual hatred of the coming of the Seed Messiah. The grief at the generations of murder on the covenant people was expressed in the prophecy "Rachel weeping for her children, refusing to be comforted..." (Jer. 31:15b). The same attack on the Jewish people because of the seed promise came to one of its most poignant moments when Herod murdered all the male children of Bethlehem at the birth of Yeshua (see Mt. 2).

The destiny of the Jewish people was to bring the Messiah child into the world. That destiny came to a pinnacle of fulfillment at the moment when Yeshua was born. The persecutions against the Jews were attacks from satan to stop the seed from being born. The birth of Yeshua can be seen as the great victory of the Jewish people over the devil. Miriam is the quintessential Jewish mama, and Yeshua the ultimate Jewish baby boy. If only more of our people could see it!

Heir of the World

When Adam sinned, God expelled him from the Garden. In some ways God had little choice but to expel Adam. By Adam's submission to the devil through sin, he had already caused a separation between himself and God, and had virtually expelled God, as it were, from planet Earth. By his sin, Adam caused himself to be expelled from the Garden of Eden.

When Adam sinned under the influence of the devil, God promised that, one day, He would bring a seed to destroy the devil. However, God could not promise Adam that He would restore the earth to him. That promise could only be made to someone who had repented, believed, and shown himself faithful. Therefore, the great seed promise had to be given in two stages: First to a sinner, then to a believer.

God promised Adam the first part, that the seed would come as a savior and destroy the devil. God then made the second half of the promise to Abraham—that through his seed, God would begin to repossess the land. Adam represents sinful man. Abraham represents the community of faith.

Genesis 12:7
Then the Lord appeared to Abram and said, "To your [seed] *I will give this land."*

Adam, as the first sinner, was told to leave Eden and go to the east. Abraham, as the first believer, was told to go west and enter the Promised Land. The return of Abraham to the Promised Land represents the beginning of the return of mankind to the Garden of Eden and the restoration of the earth.

The first words that God said to Abraham were, "Get out of your country....to a land that I will show you (see Gen. 12:1)." This statement is the reversal of God's expelling Adam from the Garden of Eden. To Adam, God's original partner, dominion over the earth was given. To Abraham, His new covenant partner, the dominion of the earth was restored.

Adam was the original owner of planet Earth. When Abraham believed, God appointed him as the new legal heir. "For the promise that he would be the heir of the world was not to Abraham or to his seed through the law, but through the righteousness of faith" (Rom. 4:13). The first seed promise was to destroy the devil. The second seed promise was to restore the earth.

As there are two promises, the work of Yeshua as the Messiah is divided into two major parts, at His two comings. At the first coming, He came for sinners—to provide a means of forgiveness for sins. At the Second Coming, Yeshua will come for the community of faith—to take dominion over the earth.

It is at this second coming that the earth will be restored, and our physical bodies will be resurrected (see Rom. 8:18-23). It is at that time that the second seed promise will be fulfilled. The first seed promise (see Gen. 3), to crush the serpent, is accepted by almost all Bible believers. Yet many have not understood the importance of the second seed promise (see Gen. 12), to inherit the land of Israel.

The Two Seed Promises

The second seed promise, concerning the possession of the land of Israel, is so important that it is repeated to all the patriarchs.

Genesis 12:7
To your [seed] *I will give this land.*
(To Abraham when he obeyed to leave his homeland.)

Genesis 13:15
All the land which you see I give to you and your [seed] *forever.*
(To Abraham when he gave up his land to Lot.)

Genesis 15:18
To your [seed] I have given this land.
(To Abraham at the covenant of the "cutting of the pieces.")

Genesis 17:8
I give to you and your [seed] *after you the land in which you are a stranger.*
(To Abraham at the covenant of the circumcision.)

Genesis 24:7
To your [seed] *I give this land.*
(When Rebecca was brought as a bride to Isaac.)

Genesis 26:3
Dwell in this land....I will give to your [seed] *all these lands.*
(During the great famine when God told Isaac not to leave the land.)

Genesis 28:13
The land on which you lie I will give to you and your [seed].
(At Bethel in Jacob's dream about the ladder.)

Genesis 35:12
The land which I gave Abraham and Isaac I give to you; and to your [seed] *after you.*
(At Bethel to Jacob when he returned from Laban.)

Genesis 48:4
I...will give this land to your descendants after you as an everlasting possession.
(To Joseph as confirmed by Jacob on his deathbed.)

This covenant to possess the land is the basis of spiritual authority by which Yeshua will return and establish His kingdom on the earth. For Yeshua to return there must be a community of faith believing in these promises. This will require a revival in Israel so that a remnant of the people there will believe in Yeshua. It will also require an understanding throughout the international Church of the importance of taking dominion over the earth and of the restoration of the land of Israel.

Types of Seed

The word for seed, zera, has three meanings in these covenants. First it refers to Yeshua as the Messianic King and Savior. Secondly it refers to the physical descendants of Abraham. Thirdly it refers to true born-again believers who have become spiritual children to Abraham (see Gal. 3:15-29).

When we speak of the physical descendants of Abraham, there are several sub-categories. In the most obvious sense, Abraham's physical descendants are the Jewish people. However, in the Old Testament, the seed referred to that part of the Jewish lineage who were carrying the seed promise—the tribe of Judah and the house of David. The genealogy ultimately passed down to Joseph and Miriam. I will call that group the *Messianic lineage*.

The Old Testament Messianic lineage held the promise of the physical birth of the Messiah. Today the seed promise is held by those Jewish people who are believers in Yeshua (see Rom. 11:5). I will call this group the *Messianic Jewish remnant*. They are the ones who will cry out, "Blessed is He who comes in the name of the Lord" when Yeshua returns (Mt. 23:39b). The Messianic remnant in our dispensation has continued the calling of the Messianic lineage from the Old Testament period.

Revelation 12:17
And the dragon was enraged with the woman, and he went to make war with the [remnant of her seed], *who keep the commandments of God and have the testimony of* [Messiah Yeshua].

The Messianic seed or remnant has a purpose in the *future* as well as the past (to be discussed in Chapter 9). The Old Testament Messianic lineage held the promise for the birth of the Messiah at the first coming. The new covenant Messianic remnant holds the promise for the return of the Messiah at the Second Coming.

O Ishmael

When we speak of the physical descendants of Abraham, we must recognize another group that is also the "seed" of Abraham. That is the Arab people. They are the physical descendants of Abraham through Ishmael. Ishmael was born of Hagar, Sarah's servant. Yet he and the nation born of him are blessed because they are also Abraham's seed.

Genesis 21:13
I will also make a nation of the son of the bondwoman, because he is your seed.

We should have a great love for the Arab peoples. As a Jew, I see them as our cousins in the Middle East. Despite the horrible conflicts that our two peoples have experienced in this century and throughout history, we should maintain the hope of reconciliation and peace that is available through Yeshua.

Abraham loved his son Ishmael. When he heard of the plan to cast out Hagar and Ishmael, he was very unhappy.

Genesis 21:11

*And the matter was very displeasing in Abraham's sight because
of his son.*

Abraham saw Ishmael as his son. When God made the covenant of circumcision, Abraham interceded for Ishmael to receive the birthright and the
blessing.

Genesis 17:18

*And Abraham said to God, "Oh, that Ishmael might live before
You!"*

God had to convince Abraham that the Messianic covenant would
come through Sarah's child.

Genesis 17:19-20

*No, Sarah your wife shall bear you a son, and you shall call his
name Isaac; I will establish My covenant with him for an everlasting covenant, and with his descendants after him.*

*And as for Ishmael, I have heard you. Behold, I have blessed
him, and will make him fruitful, and will multiply him exceedingly. He shall beget twelve princes, and I will make him a great
nation.*

Both Isaac and Ishmael were Abraham's physical seed. Both of them
were blessed because of God's favor on Abraham. Through Ishmael, the
Arabs are a blessed people. However, since there is only one Messiah, the
Messianic lineage could only come through one of Abraham's sons. That
covenant came through Isaac.

In order to protect the lineage of the Messianic seed, God had to separate the descendants of Ishmael and Isaac (see Gen. 21:12). However, that
does not restrict God's love for the Arab peoples. All of the blessings of
Abraham are for the Arabs, except for two specific aspects of the Messianic covenant: The lineage of Yeshua and the ownership of the land of Israel.

The Arabs have a rich heritage. They have preserved more of the ancient culture of the Middle East than the Jews. Their population numbers
ten times that of the Jewish people today. God has blessed them with land,
wealth, and resources.

All of the spiritual blessings of Abraham are available to Arabs
through faith in Yeshua. Not all Arabs are Muslims. Some of them have

maintained their faith in Yeshua in the midst of a hostile Muslim world. There is no group of people more beautiful in my eyes then Arab Christians.

It is God's will for Arab and Jew to be reconciled through the cross of Yeshua (see Eph. 2:14-15). Ultimately, it is God's destiny for Israel and the Arab nations to be united in His kingdom.

Isaiah 19:24-25

In that day Israel will be one of three with Egypt and Assyria—a blessing in the midst of the land,

Whom the Lord of hosts shall bless, saying, "Blessed is Egypt My people, and Assyria the work of My hands, and Israel My inheritance."

Let us pray for a mighty revival of faith in Yeshua in the Arab nations, just as we pray for Israel to be saved.

CHAPTER 7

O JERUSALEM

Everything begins in Jerusalem and ends in Jerusalem. In the biblical viewpoint, Jerusalem is the center of the world. Not only is Jerusalem the center of the world spiritually, it may also be in the place that was the center of the world physically.

The continents as we know them today were not always separated. Originally they were one large land mass. In the generation of the tower of Babel, that land mass was divided.

Genesis 10:25b
The name of one was Peleg, for in his days the earth was divided.

If you were to reconnect the continents—the Americas back to Europe and Africa, and Australia back to Southeast Asia—the earth would appear to be one land mass again. Right in the middle of that land mass would be located the "Middle East" with Jerusalem at its center.

Jerusalem and Eden

At the end of the Bible, we find new heavens and a new earth. That paradise is pictured as a restoration of the Garden of Eden. This renewed Eden has the tree of life in it again, and the rivers of pure water (see Rev. 22:1-2). This paradise is seen not only as a renewal of Eden but also as a renewal of Jerusalem.

Revelation 21:1-2
I saw a new heaven and a new earth...

I...saw the holy city, New Jerusalem, coming down out of heaven...

The perfect new world to come is seen as both a restoration of Eden and a restoration of Jerusalem. In other words, the restoration of Jerusalem is ultimately the same thing as the restoration of Eden. In biblical terms, the restoration of Jerusalem and Eden are one and the same.

If they are the same spiritually, could it be that they are the same physically? Could Jerusalem be situated in the same place where the original garden of Adam and Eve was located?

Let's start from the crucifixion and resurrection of Yeshua and work backwards. It was not a coincidence that He was crucified Jerusalem.

Luke 13:33
I must journey today, tomorrow, and the day following; for it cannot be that a prophet should perish outside of Jerusalem.

There was a reason that Yeshua had to be crucified there. Why? Because Jerusalem was the place of the temple where the sacrifices were made, and Yeshua came to fulfill the meaning of the sacrifices.

Correct. But why was the temple with the sacrifices located there? Because Jerusalem was the place where Abraham offered up Isaac as the first sacrifice.

Genesis 22:2
Take now your son, your only son Isaac, whom you love, and go to the land of Moriah, and offer him there as a burnt offering on one of the mountains of which I shall tell you.

Yeshua was offered up where the temple sacrifices were made, at a site where the "binding" of Isaac had taken place. Correct. But why was the sacrifice of Isaac located there? God directed Abraham to go to a certain place, which He *already* had in mind—there was a specific hill that He wanted to show Abraham.

The crucifixion of Yeshua, the sacrifices of the temple, and the offering of Isaac were all types of atonement for the original sin of Adam and Eve. The sin took place in the Garden of Eden. So the act of atonement had to return to "the scene of the crime" to reverse the damage. Jerusalem had to be the place for Yeshua to be crucified, because that was the place where the temple was, which was located in the place where Abraham had offered Isaac, which was the same place where the original sin of Adam and Eve took place—Eden. Jerusalem and Eden are the same place.

When Adam sinned as the first sinner, he was expelled from the Garden of Eden toward the east. When Abraham cut a covenant with God as the first believer, he was instructed to return to the Promised Land toward the west. Sin took Adam out of Eden. Faith brought Abraham back to the

Promised Land. God's first command to Abraham, the first believer, was to go back to the land of Israel.

Genesis 12:1

Get out of your country, from your family and from your father's house, to a land that I will show you.

Why is the Promised Land called the Promised Land? It is not just a place for the Jewish people to live. It is the promise that if we would come back to God in faith, He would restore us to our original way of life. It is the promise to return us to Eden. Jerusalem and the Promised Land are the promise of God to restore His kingdom and paradise to us on the earth. Jerusalem represents the promise of restoring the conditions of Eden to the earth.

Psalm 137:5-6

If I forget you, O Jerusalem, let my right hand forget its skill!

If I do not remember you, let my tongue cling to the roof of my mouth—if I do not exalt Jerusalem above my chief joy.

We must keep Jerusalem in mind, not because it is such a beautiful city, but because it represents the plan of God to restore the human race to the Garden of Eden. What we are to keep in mind is God's plan of redemption, and that plan of redemption is symbolized by Jerusalem.

Psalm 132:13

For the Lord has chosen Zion; He has desired it for His dwelling place.

Before the first sin, God dwelt with Adam and Eve in the Garden of Eden. In the new heavens and new earth, God will once again dwell with mankind in the restored Garden of Eden, the New Jerusalem (see Rev. 21:3). In this current age, Jerusalem represents the hope that one day God will dwell with mankind again. That hope we should never forget. We should always keep Jerusalem in mind. The restoration of the Kingdom of God must be our top priority.

Go West, Young Man

God expelled Adam eastward out of the Garden of Eden. God sent Abraham westward back toward the land of promise. Westward represents the direction of the Kingdom of God. God's commandment to Abraham to "get out" of his father's land (see Gen. 12:1) is in Hebrew *lech lecha*. This phrase would more literally be translated as "go ye." It is parallel to the Great Commission of Yeshua when He told His disciples, "Go ye" into all the world to preach the gospel (see Mt. 28:19; Mk. 16:15 KJV).

The preaching of the gospel and the restoration of the Promised Land are both part of bringing the Kingdom of God to the earth. As the Kingdom of God begins and ends in Jerusalem, so does the preaching of the gospel begin and end in Jerusalem. As Abraham's commission to return to the Promised Land went westward, so does the general plan for the spread of the gospel move westward.

Yeshua told His disciples to start preaching the gospel in Israel and go out to the ends of the earth (see Acts 1:8). Since the earth is round, if one starts in Jerusalem and keeps going around the world, he will end up back in Jerusalem. In the first century, as the disciples took the gospel out from Israel, they went northwest to Cyprus and north to Turkey (see Acts 11:19). [One cannot travel westward directly from Israel because of the Mediterranean Sea.]

When Paul reached Turkey he wanted to turn eastward to preach the gospel in Asia, but was forbidden by the Holy Spirit.

Acts 16:6
When they had gone through Phrygia and the region of Galatia, they were forbidden by the Holy Spirit to preach the word in Asia.

After a few days Paul received a vision that he was to preach the gospel in Greece, which of course is toward the west.

Acts 16:10
After he had seen the vision, immediately we sought to go to Macedonia, concluding that the Lord had called us to preach the gospel to them.

While the gospel spread through the disciples in every direction from Israel, the primary movement of the gospel went north into Turkey (see Rev. 2–3), and then westward into Greece. From Greece, the gospel continued westward into Rome. As the centuries went on, the gospel moved into western Europe and then, with the discovery of America, into the Western Hemisphere. In our generation the gospel has crossed over the ocean into the Far East. The largest fields of harvest now are in India and China. After that I believe the gospel will come into the Muslim world, and then finally back to Israel. Again, let me emphasize that the gospel is to be preached everywhere at all times. I am speaking here of a general pattern of the historic tide of the movement of the gospel across the nations.

India Evangelism

We have been praying for a huge sweep of evangelism in India, and believe that the time is right for a spiritual deliverance for masses of people in Hinduism there. Hinduism reinforces a horrible social discrimination called the "caste system." One of the lowest castes is the Dalits (the untouchables), in which 250 million (!) people are doomed to generations of abject poverty.

Many Dalits have come to the conclusion that the only way for their people to escape this oppression is for them to convert "en masse" to a different religion. (Christians, Muslims, and Buddhists are minorities in this Hindu nation.) At the time of this writing, some of the Dalit leaders have made contacts with Christians to help officiate in the mass conversions. While of course, that kind of conversion is not in itself a born-again experience ensuring salvation, it could very well open the door for millions of these poor Dalits to come to a real saving knowledge of Yeshua.

The Bible calls us to preach the gospel to the unsaved and to give money to the poor. India, with its hundreds of millions of both unsaved and poverty-stricken people, represents a challenge that cannot be ignored—by the civilized world in general and by born-again Christians in particular.

Korea, China, and the Far East

The Koreans are a special people. God's hand has been upon them to bring the gospel to millions of people in the Far East. There is also a significant relationship between China and Korea. Physically, Korea sits as a peninsula to the enormous Chinese land mass. There are deep historic, cultural, ethnic, and linguistic connections between the two peoples.

Beijing, China has been chosen as the site for the 2008 Olympics. This means that in the few years leading up to 2008 and continuing afterwards, China will begin to open its gates to more relationships with the international community. We are approaching an historic opportunity for the fall of communism and a massive sweep of evangelism in China.

The year 2008 may be seen as a turning point date, a target for us to focus our prayers upon. Now is the time to pray for revival in China and for the spiritual preparations for evangelism. Twenty percent of the world's population are Chinese, and sixty percent are Asians. Let us believe, pray for,

support financially, and go—that we might see in these endtimes an enormous harvest of souls in those nations.

Focal Point of Controversy

After the gospel has been preached around the world, the end will
come (see Mt. 24:14). As the gospel finishes its circuit around the world, it
will end up back in Jerusalem. When the final revival comes to Jerusalem
(see Rom. 11:26), then Yeshua will return.

Matthew 23:37,39
O Jerusalem, Jerusalem…

*You shall see me no more till you say, "Blessed is He who comes
in the name of the Lord!"*

At the Second Coming, Yeshua will return to Jerusalem.

Zechariah 14:4a
*And in that day His feet will stand on the Mount of Olives, which
faces Jerusalem on the east.*

After He comes back, He will make Jerusalem the capital and worship
center of His international kingdom.

Zechariah 14:16
*…everyone who is left of all the nations which came against
Jerusalem shall go up from year to year to worship the King…*

Since Jerusalem is the place to which Yeshua will return and set up
His kingdom, it is also the focus of spiritual conflict today. That spiritual
conflict has already caused Jerusalem to be the focal point of political
controversy.

Zechariah 12:2-3a
*I will make Jerusalem a cup of drunkenness to all the surround-
ing peoples…*

*I will make Jerusalem a very heavy stone for all peoples; all who
would heave it away will surely be cut in pieces.*

As we come closer to the second coming of Yeshua, the conflict over
Jerusalem will become more and more intense until an international war
breaks out in which the nations of the world will attack Jerusalem.

Zechariah 14:2a
I will gather all the nations to battle against Jerusalem.

At the time when the nations attack, Yeshua will intervene. That is the moment of the Second Coming. When He intervenes He will come to defend the inhabitants of Jerusalem on the one hand, and to destroy the nations that have attacked her, on the other hand.

Zechariah 12:8-9

In that day the Lord will defend the inhabitants of Jerusalem...

In that day I will seek to destroy all the nations that come against Jerusalem.

After that war Yeshua will bring world peace, starting from Jerusalem (see Is. 2). In the restoration of paradise at the very end, New Jerusalem will be the center of the new heavens and the new earth (see Rev. 21).

Jerusalem Not in Koran

Hebrew and Arabic scholar Dr. Nisim Dana recently wrote a book discussing the fact that Jerusalem is not mentioned even once in the Koran. This claim is important because the conflict in the Middle East is based on the religious claims of Islam that Jerusalem is "holy" territory for Muslims. These claims are, in turn, supposed to be based on the Koran, which is the final authority in Islam.

If Jerusalem is not mentioned in the Koran, then the claims of Islam over Jerusalem have no direct authority. Those claims are based on later teachings of sheiks and imams without textual support from the Koran.

The Koran itself takes for granted that Jewish habitation of the land of Israel is not only not against Muhammad's teaching, but, in fact, a divine commandment from Allah. Professor Dana quotes several passages of the Koran supporting this view (Sura 5:21; Sura 7:137). Sura 17 contains an interesting quote: "and Allah said to the children of Israel: Dwell in the Land, and when the time of the end days comes, we will gather you tribe by tribe."

According to Dana, Jerusalem is also indirectly referred to (Sura 2:142) when Muhammad cancels the biblical commandment for the nations of the world to face toward Jerusalem in prayer. It is significant to note that when Muslims pray in Jerusalem, they turn their backs toward the Temple Mount and face Mecca.

There is a story in Islamic tradition that Muhammad ascended on a white horse from Jerusalem to Heaven after his death. This story is not found in the Koran, but only became part of Islamic folklore in later sources. Most early Islamic commentators considered that story spurious.

Professor Dana even quotes from the biography of Ayisha, Muhammad's beloved wife, as saying that Muhammad's corpse was with her in the house, and that Allah simply took his soul to Heaven. The only possible verse that has any remote connection in the Koran (Sura 17) is "blessed be He who brought His servant at night from the holy sanctuary to the outermost sanctuary." The words here "outermost sanctuary" are "misgad Al Aqsa," which in later times was connected to the Al Aqsa mosque in Jerusalem.

How could it happen that millions of Muslims are ready to declare Jihad on Israel, and thousands of Palestinians ready to become suicide terrorists in order to liberate the holy city of Jerusalem, when Jerusalem is not even mentioned in the Koran? The answer is probably that most Muslims do not actually read the Koran for themselves.

The people are assuming that the Islamic clerics are basing their teachings on the authority of the Koran. As the sheiks and imams urge them towards Jihad against Israel, they assume that this Jihad is a divine commandment. (The only connection between Jihad and Jews is a passage in which Jihad was declared against a group of Jews living in Medina, Saudi Arabia, who refused to accept Muhammad as their prophet; the passage had nothing to do with Israel.)

The fervent religious claims that Jerusalem is holy territory to Islam can only have force (even if incorrect) if they are based on direct commandments of Muhammad. I wish I could put up a billboard in every Muslim city and town, saying, "Jerusalem is not mentioned in the Koran even one time." Without the authority of the Koran, Islamic claims concerning Israel lose their power.

Jerusalem Comes Down

Many Christians do not see any relevance to the city of Jerusalem, because they see Jerusalem only as a heavenly dwelling place. To illustrate the point, I am reminded of a story related by Thomas Friedman in his book *From Beirut to Jerusalem*, about Simcha Dinitz, former Israeli ambassador to the United States. Dinitz delivered a lecture to a black church in Washington D.C. in the early 1960s. "After my talk," said Dinitz, "a young girl came up to me and said, 'Where do you live?' I said, 'Jerusalem.' She thought about that for a minute and said, 'Jerusalem, is that a place on earth? I thought it was in heaven.'"

There is a heavenly Jerusalem. However, three times the Book of Revelation states that heavenly Jerusalem descends from Heaven. To the faithful at the congregation at Philadelphia, considered to be the best of all the congregations, is promised:

Revelation 3:12b

I will write on him the name of My God and the name of the city of My God, the New Jerusalem, which comes down out of heaven from My God...

At the founding of the new heaven and new earth at the end of the Millennium, John foresees the New Jerusalem as well.

Revelation 21:2-3

...the holy city New Jerusalem, coming down out of heaven from God, prepared as a bride adorned for her husband.

And I heard a loud voice from heaven saying, "Behold, the tabernacle of God is with men, and He will dwell with them, and they shall be His people...

The Jerusalem of above is the dwelling place of all the angels who remained loyal to God, and of the spirits of godly men and women who have passed away. Since the international community of believers in Yeshua is called the Bride of Messiah (see Eph. 5), then so is heavenly Jerusalem called here a bride, since that is where the people live.

The descent of New Jerusalem is seen as a joining together of the dwelling places of God and man into one. Most of Revelation chapter 21 is dedicated to describing this heavenly dwelling place. It is the final restoration of the Garden of Eden, the ultimate marriage of the Lamb, and the total reconciliation between God and mankind.

Revelation 21:10

And he carried me away in the Spirit to a great and high mountain, and showed me the great city, the holy Jerusalem, descending out of heaven from God.

The New Testament idea that there is a heavenly Jerusalem is similar to the rabbinic idea that there are two Jerusalems, one "of above" and one "of below." (There is also a tabernacle in Heaven and a courtroom of Heaven that are parallel to the tabernacle and "Sanhedrin" here below.)

When a godly person "passes away," his body goes into the grave and his spirit rises into this heavenly city called Jerusalem. There he will stay until it is time for him to receive his resurrection body. Then those godly people living in the heavenly Jerusalem will descend and pick up their earthly bodies, resurrected to be able to live forever in the restored paradise of the Garden of Eden.

This is the dwelling place described by Yeshua in John's gospel:

John 14:2-3

In My Father's house are many mansions...

If I go and prepare a place for you, I will come again and receive you to Myself...

So there the righteous will live with Yeshua and God. At the time of the new creation, that heavenly dwelling place comes down. If it comes down, there must be a place upon which it will come to rest. That place is on earth. Its center is Jerusalem.

The righteous will always be in Jerusalem. First they will be in the Jerusalem that is in Heaven, and then in the Jerusalem that comes down to be part of the new heaven and earth that will be restored on the earth. So yes, certainly the spirits of the righteous go up into Heaven when they die. But ultimately, their dwelling place will be back here on earth as that heavenly Jerusalem comes down.

CHAPTER 8

INTIFADA

By the summer of 2000, the Camp David talks with Clinton, Barak, and Arafat were in full swing. Ehud Barak, the most decorated soldier in modern Israeli history, had set himself to negotiate a peace settlement with Arafat by putting all the issues on the table. He had just completed a unilateral withdrawal of Israeli forces from southern Lebanon. While there were objections from the right that the withdrawal would be interpreted by the Arabs as weakness, and therefore encourage more terrorism, it received widespread approval in Israeli public opinion.

Barak, riding this wave of success and popularity, offered to give back or remove Israeli presence from the disputed territories, allow for a Palestinian state with its capital in East Jerusalem, and even relinquish control over the Temple Mount area! The right wing went into panic. The mainstream was confused. Even the left wing was amazed at how far Barak was pushing. It seemed crazy. But… who knows? Israel was so tired of the wars and the struggles. Perhaps if we just made concessions on all the issues, we could get to peace.

One thing that Barak demanded was an "end of conflict" clause. In other words, that the Arab world would agree to this treaty and commit to no further demands being made on Israel. Here Arafat balked. The talks started to stall.

Sharon's Visit

The right wing felt the need to move. A year earlier the Likud party under the leadership of then prime minister Benjamin Netanyahu, suffered a severe defeat at the hands of the Labor party under Barak. The new chairman of the Likud party, Ariel Sharon, decided to protest by making an official "visit" to the Temple Mount. The visit, of course, would be a statement of Jewish rights to the Temple Mount area.

He invited Knesset members from all parties to join him. Actually very few showed up. While on the Temple Mount, although accompanied by heavy security, Sharon was pelted by rocks. Violent demonstrations erupted all over the Palestinian territories. The response was much greater than anyone (on the Israeli side) expected. Barak, frustrated by Arafat's intransigence, publicly backed Sharon's right to visit the Temple Mount, although not agreeing to the particular timing of the event.

The situation, instead of quieting down over the next few weeks, grew worse. The Camp David talks collapsed with both sides walking out in anger. At that point, Arafat proclaimed the opening of a new "Intifada," a civil uprising or terrorist war against Israel.

The Israeli public was stunned. Despite the rhetoric against the concessions that Barak was offering, it was likely that a plebiscite vote would have affirmed the treaty. The Israeli public so desperately wanted peace, that it was ready for anything, even what seemed to be humiliating and dangerous concessions. But Arafat refused. He not only refused; he opened a war in return.

Within a few weeks, Barak's government was toppled. Sharon became the new prime minister. Even more disconcerting than the change in government was the shaking of the Israeli worldview. The very conception that it would be possible ever to negotiate and arrive at a peaceful agreement was deeply undermined.

And the Intifada continued and continued. Almost all the Palestinians working in Israeli businesses were fired. Laborers from China, Romania, the Philippines, and Nigeria were brought in to cover the jobs. Tourism to Israel dropped to virtually zero. That caused a chain effect in other related businesses, such as hotels and restaurants. Foreign investment also dropped dramatically. Unemployment in Israel skyrocketed. With the high costs of prolonging a war that seemed to go on and on, there was no budget left for schools, hospitals, and welfare.

The police were so stretched in security issues that crime protection went down. The despair of the people began to express itself in symptoms of higher sexual abuse, violence in families, gambling, and substance abuse.

And on the Palestinian side, the disaster was almost total. Widespread malnutrition, poverty, and unemployment ruined the day-to-day life of the average Palestinian. The Palestinian authority was plagued with horrible financial corruption, so that donations from Europe and the Arab nations never reached the people. Militant fanatic Islam spread more and more. A subculture idolizing terror grew up that gripped large parts of the Palestinian youth and even children. Arafat at one point even called for a "million suicide terrorists" to volunteer to "liberate" Jerusalem.

When Sharon was elected as prime minister, he wanted to alter his image as hard right wing. He offered to open negotiations by declaring a unilateral cease-fire on Israel's part. Arafat continued the Intifada. After the World Trade Center disaster, another attempt was made to negotiate a cease-fire, to no avail.

What Arafat Sees

How could it have been that Arafat turned down Barak's peace offer? Why did he declare an Intifada war against Israel, which would wreak such damage on his own people? Why did he reject Israel's offer of a cease-fire when Sharon was first elected? Why did he refuse to take a stand against terrorism after the World Trade Center disaster? Why has he used international donations to foster the culture of suicide terrorism instead of seeking to improve his people's socio-economic condition?

Do Arafat and the leaders of the Islamic terrorist groups, like Hamas, Jihad, and Hizbollah see something we don't see?

Arafat believes that millions of Muslims worldwide will stand with him in a Jihad to "liberate" the "holy land" of "Palestine." He believes that through propaganda and media, he can persuade the European community and most of the "third-world" nations either to support him, or at least to raise no objection. He believes that American society and the international Christian community, while sympathizing with Israel, will be neutralized through cowardice, indecision, or passivity. He believes that the pluralistic, democratic society in Israel will be divided against itself and unable to stand.

In short, he sees more in his favor than against him. He believes he can win this Jihad against Israel. To a certain degree, he is correct.

Zechariah 14:2

I will gather all the nations to battle against Jerusalem; the city shall be taken, the houses rifled, and the women [raped]...

Yes, according to the Bible, the combined Islamic Jihad and the United Nations attack against Israel will win. Let's look at the balance of power.

Israel is stronger than the Palestinians. However, the Islamic nations together with the Palestinians are stronger than Israel. The United States together with Israel are stronger than the Islamic nations with the Palestinians. However, the coalition of the United Nations and the Islamic nations are stronger than Israel and the United States. That's the part that Arafat sees. That's why he sees himself as the victor.

While Arafat sees the victory of that great apocalyptic Jihad and international coalition against Israel, there is another part he does not see.

Zechariah 14:3-4a,12

Then the Lord will go forth and fight against those nations, as He fights in the day of battle.

And in that day His feet will stand on the Mount of Olives.

And this shall be the plague with which the Lord will strike all the people who fought against Jerusalem: their flesh shall dissolve while they stand on their feet, their eyes shall dissolve in their sockets, and their tongues shall dissolve in their mouths.

The victory of the combined forces against Israel will be short lived. The Apocalypse is interrupted. The battle of Armageddon is not won by the international coalition, but by the intervention of the coming of the Messiah. The forces that attack Israel will be horribly destroyed, and then true peace will begin. Yeshua as King of the Jews will return to Jerusalem to set up His kingdom.

That's the part the Muslim leaders don't see. For that matter, neither do most of the Christians and Jews.

What's It All About?

The terrorist attacks of fundamentalist Islam are aimed at three targets primarily: the United States, Israel, and Christian missionaries. The United States is considered the most Christian nation on earth. Israel is the homeland of the Jews. Missionaries help spread the gospel in non-Christian areas. What is the common denominator?

The link between the three is the Second Coming. Yeshua will return soon to set up His kingdom on the earth. The place where He will do this is Jerusalem.

Terrorist attacks are not normal; they are inhuman. An evil spiritual force propels them. Terrorist attacks are certainly demonically inspired. But what is the devil's goal in these attacks? What is the purpose of satan in focusing these attacks on Israel and the Christian world?

It is to try to stop the second coming of Yeshua. That's what the devil is afraid of. Why? Because at Yeshua's return, the devil will be thrown in the abyss. It is his end and he knows it.

Revelation 20:1-3

I saw an angel coming down from heaven, having the key to the bottomless pit and a great chain in his hand.

He laid hold of the dragon, that serpent of old, who is the Devil and Satan, and bound him for a thousand years;

And he cast him into the bottomless pit, and shut him up, and set a seal on him, so that he should deceive the nations no more till the thousand years were finished...

This is what scares satan. The primary concern of the devil is not that people will become believers in Yeshua and go to Heaven. Let them go. He still rules on earth. He is interested in protecting his turf on this planet. He wants to stop the return of Yeshua, which spells his defeat. All evil in the world is focused on one thing: stopping the Second Coming.

And the place on earth that Yeshua will return to is Israel. If there is no Israel, there is no Second Coming. Yeshua's return to Israel does not mean a return to an empty desert, but to a restored nation of Israel, a Jewish homeland after the two-thousand-year punishment of the exile.

He is not coming to an Islamic nation of "Palestine." He is coming back as King of the Jews to His people. From there He will reign. That's why above the cross it was written, "King of the Jews." Even while being crucified, Yeshua promised that He would return as King of the Jews. That sign above His head was a prophecy of His second coming. It was an eternal statement of His identity and authority.

Israel is the Holy Land not because it is the place where Jesus walked two millennia ago. It is the Holy Land because it is where He will walk in the Millennium when He returns. It is not a coincidence that bin Laden's primary reason for attacking America, as he has announced several times on video, is that the United States dares to support Israel's occupation of "Islamic Holy Land." The purpose of terrorism against America is to scare Americans away from standing with Israel.

If Israel is Islamic Holy Land, then Yeshua cannot come back, and the devil will not be destroyed. The devil is fighting to save his own skin. The connection between Yeshua and Jerusalem is what will destroy him. That is the purpose behind Islamic terror, just as it was the purpose behind Nazi holocaust. If Israel is a secular atheist country that hates God, or a country controlled by a rabbinic Judaism that hates Yeshua, then the Second Coming is likewise thwarted.

The Three Enemies

Therefore, the satanic strategy to stop the return of Yeshua has, by its very nature, these three lines of attack: The terrorism of Islamic fundamentalism against Israel, the lusts of the secular humanistic world to weaken the Church, and the rejection of Yeshua by rabbinic Judaism against the movement of Jewish believers in Yeshua. I am not speaking here of militant Islam, liberal humanism or rabbinic Judaism per se, but rather of certain spiritual forces operating through them. Those three spiritual enemies are suicide terrorism, the lusts of this world, and religious rejection of Yeshua.

Those three spiritual enemies were highlighted to me once during a summer musical outreach here in Israel directed by "Souled Out" Ministries from Chicago. Many of the Israeli Messianic youth, both teens and young adults, were involved. One night in Netanya, Eitan Shishkoff (leader of congregation "Ohalei Rachamim" in Haifa) and I were serving as both parents and pastoral overseers. The outreach was wonderful.

At the same time we were praying for their protection. First, since it was a crowded public square, there was the danger of a terrorist attack. Secondly, because they were sharing their faith, there was the danger of persecution from the ultra-orthodox. Thirdly, because they were teenagers, there was the danger from the influence of secular Israeli culture, filled with sexual immorality, drug use, etc.

These three battle fronts must be faced every day. Many of the Israeli Messianic youth serve in the Israeli army, protecting the citizens from terrorist attacks. Believers around the world, who serve either in law enforcement or in third-world missions, have to face similar life threatening situations. Whether from the communist regime in China, militant Muslims in Indonesia, drug cartels in Columbia, or organized crime in the inner cities, believers who choose to stand up for righteousness will have to face threats on their very lives.

Secondly, we note that the strongest opposition to Yeshua's ministry was not from the sinners, but from the religious leaders and hypocrites. He even referred to them as snakes and vipers (see Mt. 23:33). Recently I was out sharing the gospel on the streets of Tel Aviv. One of the ultra-orthodox "anti-missionaries" came to harass me. He began to hiss at me. He cursed me over one hundred times in an ugly tone of voice saying, "You're going to burn in hell, you're going to burn in hell, you're going to burn in hell." (When he finished, I simply danced a little jig in the street in the spirit of Luke 6:23.)

Thirdly, the modern Western world is being flooded by spirits of sexual immorality. Essentially it is a spirit of adultery. This spirit weakens the faith of believers in Yeshua wherever they are found. It robs us of our holiness. It has made many in the community of faith to be like Samson asleep on the knees of Delilah (see Judg. 16:19). (The name *Delilah* comes from the Hebrew root that means "dilute." The spirit of immorality dilutes the spiritual strength of those who otherwise could have been great heroes of faith.)

I see the spirit of sexual immorality in the world in these endtimes being symbolized by the figure of the "great whore" of the Book of Revelation chapters 17–18. I see the spirit of violence and terrorism being symbolized by the figure of the "beast" in the Book of Revelation chapter 13. The spirit of the beast has been found in many different forms throughout history.

One of the common factors of this violence is a spirit of revenge, particularly combined with a sense of having been treated unfairly (having been "ripped off"). Cain murdered Abel because he saw God's blessings on Abel and was jealous. He thought he had been treated unfairly by God and sought revenge. The same may be said of Ishmael's reaction to Isaac, and Esau's reaction to Jacob. In fact this spirit of revenge has come through many generations.

Ezekiel 35:5

Because you have had an ancient hatred, and have shed the blood of the children of Israel by the power of the sword...

We are not against Arabs, but against the spirit of terrorism. We are not against Jews, but against the spirit of rejection of Yeshua. We are not against

Western society, but against the spirits of lust and immorality so rampant there.

The rejection of Yeshua by religious leaders and hypocrites is also mirrored throughout the Old Testament in the attacks upon the prophets. Joseph's brothers tried to kill him (see Gen. 37). The people of Israel almost stoned Moses (see Ex. 17:4). Saul's men tried to kill David; the kings of Israel tried to kill Elijah and Elisha; the leaders of Judah almost killed Jeremiah; and they actually did kill Zechariah the son of Yehoiada (see 2 Chron. 24:21).

If we are to be strong in our faith, we must stand against crime and terrorism, against lust and immorality, and against religious persecution of all kinds.

Islam, the United Nations, and the Second Coming

The fact that the second coming of Yeshua is connected with a battle over Jerusalem (see Zech. 14:2) raises several theological problems. Interestingly enough, the strange combination of terrorism, Islam, and the United Nations is shedding light on how this prophecy could come to pass.

The first problem is one of *coalition*: How could all the nations of the world, from so many different backgrounds, come together in agreement? Over recent years we have seen the bloc of Islamic nations joining together with the liberal humanist nations of Europe in anti-Israel resolutions in the United Nations. Although the European humanists and the religious Muslims are so different in their worldviews, they are able to come into unity against Israel.

The second problem is one of *focus*: How could all the nations of the world be focused against one small nation? Here again we see the combined influence of terrorism, Islam, and the United Nations. Terrorism affects all the nations of the world, but its primary focus is Jerusalem. Islamic claims on Jerusalem as its holy city (Al Quds) and the Palestinian anti-Israel propaganda in the United Nations have already made Jerusalem the focal point of international conflict.

The third problem is one of *Christian eschatology*: How are Christians around the world to equate their faith in Jesus with the city of Jerusalem? Certainly a Christian well-read in the prophecies of the Bible will be aware that the battles of the endtimes are centered around Jerusalem. However, modern events are also forcing Christians to see the connection between Jesus and Israel. As some Christians see in the United

Nations the beginning of a one-world antichristian government, so do they see the United Nations as a forum for anti-Israel propaganda. As Islam has become in our generation the primary obstacle to world evangelism, so has it become the primary instigator of attacks against Israel. Militant Islamic terrorism is not only directed gainst Jews; it is also the greatest cause of Christian martyrdom in the world today.

The fourth problem is one of *Jewish messianic expectations*: While many religious Jews understand biblical prophecy about the coming of the Messiah at the time of a great apocalyptic battle over Jerusalem, they do not see the prophecy as connected with Yeshua. However, as the nations of the world turn more against Jerusalem, the people of Israel will find that their only allies are staunchly evangelical Christians. I am reminded of a morning talk show recently on the largest Israeli television station. I heard a perplexed discussion as to how it could be that the only people really standing with Israel are the radical religious right of evangelical Christianity. Unfortunately, they totally misunderstood this phenomenon as being a strange form of Christian anti-Semitism. However, the awareness of the phenomenon (of the support of Israel by evangelical Christians) is already well-noted in Israel.

The fifth problem is one of *morality*: If Yeshua is coming back to judge the world in righteousness (see Ps. 98:13), why would He punish those who are against Israel? After all, Israel is no more righteous than any other nation. Where is the morality in that? There are many evils in the world today. Yet suicide terrorism has become the greatest of them all. We have yet to see the effects of what suicide terrorists will do if they can get their hands on small nuclear devices or biological/chemical weapons.

Suicide terrorism will become the issue that forms a moral dividing line between good and evil. Every moral person will have to take a stand against terrorism. Since the number one focus of worldwide terrorism is Jerusalem, Jerusalem will, by necessity, de facto, become a moral dividing line as well.

Liberal humanism in the United Nations, religious militancy in Islam, and the new wave of suicide terrorism are forcing Christians, the people of Israel, and moral people everywhere to draw closer together. This alignment sets the stage for the prophecies concerning the second coming of Yeshua to take place.

Faithful Unto Death

Victory in the endtimes is connected to purity and to being faithful unto death. While the devil is out to stop the Second Coming, we are serving to bring Yeshua back. In order to do that, we have to see a mobilizing of the parts of God's plan.

There will be an increasing call to holiness and repentance within the Church. The doctrines that remove holiness and repentance from the gospel have weakened the community of faith. Repentance is one of the foundations of faith. We are called not just to believe, but to "Repent and believe…" (see Mk. 1:15; Acts 2:38; Rom. 1:5).

Every believer must know how to walk in the authority he has in Yeshua. Yeshua has given us power to bind and loose spiritual forces in His name (see Mt. 16:19). We have victory in our faith (see 1 Jn. 5:4); we have authority over all power of the devil (see Lk. 10:19); we have authority in the name of Yeshua to heal the sick and do miracles (Acts 4:10). The Book of Revelation tells of our final victory over the forces of evil.

Revelation 12:11
They overcame [the accuser] *by the blood of the Lamb and by the word of their testimony, and they did not love their lives to the death.*

However, the victory that we have in the name of Yeshua comes into action as we have a commitment to be faithful to Him even unto the death. There will be many martyrs in the endtimes (see Rev. 2:10; 15:2). Our faithfulness unto death is an integral part of our victory. There will be a new breed of believers who will go all the way to be conformed to the image of Yeshua even unto death (see Phil. 2:8; 3:10). A special place of leadership and authority in the world to come is given to those who have served the Lord unto martyrdom (see Rev. 20:4).

CHAPTER 9

THE REMNANT

If the Church is to stand with Israel in the endtimes, the theology of "Church replacement" must be rooted out. Church replacement is correct in the sense that the international community of faith has carried on the covenant of ancient Israel, while most of the nation of Israel has been apostate. However, that does not mean that the Church has replaced Israel in the sense that God's purposes for Israel have ended.

Romans 11:1-2,11

I say then, has God cast away His people? Certainly not!...

God has not cast away His people who He foreknew...

I say then, have they stumbled that they should fall? Certainly not!...

The gospel was originally brought to the gentile nations by the first Jewish apostles of Yeshua. This was part of God's design, so that in the end the gentile church could bring the gospel back to the Jewish people.

Romans 11:11,13-14

...through their fall, to provoke them to jealousy, salvation has come to the Gentiles.

I speak to you Gentiles; inasmuch as I am an apostle to the Gentiles, I magnify my ministry,

If by any means I may provoke to jealousy those who are my flesh and save some of them.

The Church is not to believe that Israel has been replaced, but rather that Israel will be restored. We should believe in Israel's restoration, not her replacement. Israel's restoration will bring about the second coming of Yeshua, the resurrection of the dead, and the next stage of the Kingdom of God.

Romans 11:12,15

If their fall is riches for the world, and their failure riches for the Gentiles, how much more their fullness!

If their being cast away is the reconciling of the world, what will their acceptance be but life from the dead?

Most Jewish people, because of their rejection of Yeshua, have been like branches cut off of their own tree. The gentile church has been like branches grafted into the tree of faith (see Rom. 11:16-22). However, we are to believe that the Jewish people will return and be grafted into the faith of their own Messiah—the most spiritually "natural" thing for them to do.

Romans 11:23

They also, if they do not continue in unbelief, will be grafted in, for God is able to graft them in again.

Not only is God able to bring the Jewish people back to faith in Yeshua, He has promised that He will do so.

Romans 11:26a

And so all Israel will be saved.

Notice the words "and so" in this verse. It's not just that all Israel will be saved, but that *something* will happen which will lead to that salvation. What is that something which leads to the "and so"? It is the change in the attitude of the Church toward Israel's destiny:

Romans 11:25

For I do not desire, brethren, that you should be ignorant of this mystery, lest you should be wise in your own opinion, that blindness in part has happened to Israel until the fullness of the Gentiles has come in. And so...

As the Church receives the revelation of the end-times restoration of Israel, it will pave the way for Israel to come to salvation, which in turn will lead to the second coming of Yeshua.

In the meantime, we have a paradoxical position toward the Jewish people who have not yet received the Lord. It is part negative and part positive.

Romans 11:28

Concerning the gospel they are enemies for your sake, but concerning the election they are beloved for the sake of the fathers.

On the one hand we have to resist the enmity in our people against the gospel. Our people have been at the core of the resistance to the gospel. On the other hand, the calling of God on the nation of Israel in bringing about the Kingdom of God is irrevocable.

Romans 11:29
For the gifts and the calling of God are irrevocable.

Despite the sin and stubbornness of our people, the calling upon the nation remains the same.

The Remnant Within Israel

I have a great love for the body of Messianic believers in Israel, which I see as the spiritual remnant of the nation of Israel. The very existence of this remnant has great prophetic significance.

The general body of believers in Israel has three parts. The first is the international Christian community. This is made up of people from every denomination and ethnic group in the world, living in Israel primarily on visa status. Israel as the "Holy Land" is a second home to Christians everywhere. As Messianic Jews, we realize that true born-again Christians are our spiritual brothers and sisters.

The second part of the body of believers in Israel is the Palestinian Christians. This group is dear to us in a special way. They live in the difficult circumstances of being almost overwhelmed by the militant Islamic culture around them, and torn by the political conflict between the Israelis and the Palestinians. They are heroes in the faith and carry with them God's destiny for all the Arab peoples.

The third group is the Messianic Jews, those who are Israeli citizens, Jewish and believers in Yeshua. This group currently numbers around seven thousand. It is this group that I am primarily identified with. I believe they have a key role to play in the Kingdom of God.

In A.D. 70, the nation of Israel was sent into exile as punishment from God (see Lk. 21:24; 19:42). Since the plan of redemption in the Bible is presented through God's covenants with the people of Israel, the destruction of the nation presents a theological conflict. Within the traditional Jewish faith, the issues of exile and redemption (*galut* and *geulah*) are major concerns. As the faith in Yeshua spread to the gentile nations in the first century, the exile of Israel presented a problem to the early Christians as well. This is the question that Paul addresses in Romans chapters 9–11.

We know that Paul's answer to the question whether the prophetic purposes of Israel have been made void is, "Certainly not!" (see Rom. 11:1). But how could the destiny of Israel *not* be canceled, considering the rejection of the Messiah and the punishment from God? Here Paul's answer is also clear: *The remnant.*

Throughout history there was always a minority of true believers within the greater nation of Israel. Despite the sins of the nation, that believing remnant carried within it (in seed form) the divine destiny of the nation.

Every nation, in fact, has a prophetic calling from God. That calling is not seen in the overall population of the nation, but in the community of true believers found within the nation. The prophetic calling of the United States is not seen in motion pictures from Hollywood. That of South Africa is not seen in the racial problems; of Germany, not in Nazism; of Russia, not in communism, etc. The destiny of a nation and its covenant with God are found within the remnant of believers within the nation.

The same is true in Israel. The source of its destiny is not in Tel Aviv discos, nor political parties, nor rabbinic councils. It is in Yeshua, and in the community of citizens that believe in Him. If one wants to understand the destiny of Israel, he must look not to the larger unbelieving population of Israel, but to the core community of believers within the nation. Gentile Christians become confused by not making this distinction. Either they reject God's purposes for Israel altogether, or they try to make something overly spiritual of Israel's pioneers and politicians.

Romans 9:6

They are not all Israel who are of Israel.

Some people are "of Israel" (physically) but not Israel (in the spiritual sense). That is, many of the overall population of Israel are not part of the Israel of faith. However there are some who are both—not everyone, but some.

In many ways, the Messianic Jews are the weakest element within Israeli society (see 1 Cor. 1:26). We have few leaders yet in government, business, or the arts. Many Messianic Jews are socially estranged, financially oppressed, and often psychologically damaged. Yet, by the grace of God, His light and the very hope of our nation are found in our midst.

The way to have a balanced theology concerning Israel and its destiny is to consider the Messianic Jewish community within Israel. Paul wrote that the way to understand God's plan for Israel was to compare the faithful remnant in the time of Elijah to the Messianic Jewish community of his day.

Romans 11:2,4-5

God has not cast away His people whom He foreknew. Or do you not know what the Scripture says of Elijah...

What does the divine response say to him? "I have reserved for Myself seven thousand men who have not bowed the knee to Baal."

Even so then, at this present time there is a remnant according to the election of grace.

Even so as it was in the time of Elijah, so it is today. The destiny of Israel, God's plan for the nation, is found within the remnant. Even Elijah was confused when he saw that such a huge majority of the nation of Israel were not believers. However, God told him not to look at the unbelieving majority, but at the believing minority.

In Elijah's time, in Paul's time, and even so *at this present time*—there was a remnant and there still is a remnant. And how many are in that remnant? Seven thousand.

In the time of Elijah, there was a remnant of seven thousand believers within Israel who carried with them the destiny of the nation. Today there is also a remnant within Israel numbering about seven thousand. This remnant is part of bringing us to a new "age of Elijah" in our generation. God had to point out to Elijah the importance of the seven thousand faithful ones. The revelation of the remnant gave him hope, faith, and a better understanding of God's purpose. I believe God is trying to point out the importance of the Messianic remnant within Israel today as well.

The Two Witnesses

Revelation 11 speaks of two great end-times prophets, called "the two witnesses." An image of these two is seen in the two olive branches that give anointing oil to the lampstand in Zechariah 4. A further image is found in the two pillars that stand by the opening of the Temple of Solomon (see 1 Kings 8).

Many people waste far too much time speculating on *who* these two witnesses are. The more important question is *what* they have to say. Their job is to point the way toward the second coming of Yeshua, just as John the

Baptist pointed the way to His first coming. John said, "He's the one who is important, not me" (see John 3).

Dan Juster, Messianic theologian and director of Tikkun Ministries, points out in *The Passover Key* that the two witnesses challenge the "antichrist" in much the same way that Aaron and Moses challenged Pharaoh. As John the Baptist was beheaded for rebuking sin, so these two witnesses will be martyred.

Although there are two individual men who are referred to as the two witnesses, it is worth noting that the primary two witnesses of God throughout history are the international Church and the nation of Israel. Israel and the Church are the two prophetic bodies ordained by God to witness of His purposes.

The two pillars of Solomon's Temple had names: Boaz and Yachin. *Boaz* means "strength is in him," and refers to Yeshua, in whom the fullness of God dwells in bodily form (see Col. 2:9). *Yachin* means "he will prepare (or establish)." This also refers to Yeshua, whose job it is as Messiah to establish God's predestined plan on the earth. *Boaz* refers to the incarnation; *Yachin* to God's sovereignty.

However, the name *Boaz* also refers to an historical figure known in the Book of Ruth. The story of Ruth and Boaz has a symbolic meaning, in which Ruth may be seen as the Church coming out of the gentile nations to be married to Boaz, who is a figure of the Messiah.

The very existence of the international community of faith is a supernatural phenomenon that bears witness to the purposes of God (see Eph. 2:7; 3:10). People all over the world, from every different country, have risen above their pagan cultures to believe in the one true God and in His Messiah.

However, Ruth not only married Boaz, she also joined her destiny to that of the people of Israel. Similarly the Church has not only "married" Yeshua, they have also joined their destiny with the people of Israel.

The end-times community of faith will say along with Ruth, "Your people shall be my people" (Ruth 1:16). That evangelical Christians all over the world are expressing their identification with the nation of Israel is one of the signposts that Yeshua is about to return. As Christians look forward to the return of Yeshua to Jerusalem, they will find themselves identifying more and more with the nation of Israel.

The prophetic call for the community of faith to recognize the place of Israel is not a racist preference for the Jewish people, but rather a submission to the sovereignty of God. It is a recognition of Jerusalem as the seat of His earthly authority and a recognition of Yeshua as King of the Jews.

Yet how can the Church be covenanted to Israel, when Israel has rejected her Messiah? The answer is that the covenant link to Israel as a nation is through the believing remnant within Israel (see Rom. 11:1-5). The Messianic believers are a spiritual bridge between the international Church and the nation of Israel.

Therefore the Messianic remnant within Israel is also a kind of Boaz figure. In a certain sense the international Church (Ruth) is also to be married to the Messianic remnant within Israel (Boaz). In that marriage, there is a recognition of biblical order and priestly authority. It is like a woman submitting to her husband, or like younger brothers recognizing the right of the firstborn. The international community of faith is pictured as a family of nations with the remnant of Israel as the older brother (see Ex. 4:22; Hos. 11:1). The Church is pictured as married not only to Yeshua, but also to the people of Israel (see Eph. 2:14-15).

Ruth is the hero of the Book of Ruth, not Boaz. In a parallel way the international community of faith is more "spiritual" than Israel. It will take a great faith and humility for the Church to see her connection with Israel and with the remnant within Israel (see Rom. 11:25).

The name *Yachin* is a shortened form of "Yehoiachin," who is also an historical figure. He was the king of Judah who was taken captive by Nebuchadnezzar at the time of the Babylonian exile. After many years in captivity, Yehoiachin was released and returned to a position of honor and authority (see 2 Kings 25:27-30).

Yehoiachin's captivity and release are symbolic of the death and resurrection of Yeshua. Thus, the Yachin figure points to Yeshua, who likewise was cut off and then reestablished as king.

Yet the captivity and release of Yehoichin also points to the exile and regathering of the Jewish people. The reestablishment of the nation of Israel is an unprecedented phenomenon in world history and an undeniable testimony of the sovereignty of God. It is something that God had "prepared" and "established" in His sovereignty.

If Yeshua is to return to take up His throne as the king of Israel, there must be a throne for Him to return to. There must be a structure of government in Israel that will form the base of Yeshua's kingdom. Yeshua's authority is heavenly now, but it will soon be incarnate into real government in this world (see Jn. 18:36).

Yet how can the governing authorities in Israel form a base of Yeshua's earthly authority, if the nation does not believe in Him? One answer is simply for the gospel to be preached in this land. That's our top priority (see Rom. 9:1-3; 1 Cor. 9:20-22). We must share the gospel at all costs, both in Israel and around the world.

Messianic believers are taking up places of authority within Israeli society. Some are officers in the Israeli army. A few are in law, medicine, education, and the arts—not many, but this is just the beginning. As Messianic Jews gain these kinds of positions, a framework of authority and government will be reestablished in the land.

The ministry of the two witnesses prepares the way for Yeshua's return to earth. Their messages deal with the establishment of godly authority on the earth—in the Church, in Israel, and in the Messianic remnant. Their prophecies will complete the mystery of God and result in the kingdoms of this world being taken over and transformed by the kingdom of Yeshua (see Rev. 11:15).

There Is a Time

Yeshua's first-century disciples asked Him if He would restore the kingdom to Israel at that time.

Acts 1:6b-7

"Lord, will You at this time restore the kingdom to Israel?"

And He said to them, "It is not for you to know the times or seasons which the Father has put in His own authority."

Yeshua said that it was not the time then. If the time was not then, there must be a time. If He said that it was not for them to know the times, then there must be a time. I would like to ask this question again in our generation. Is it the time now to restore the kingdom to Israel?

We are not to be concerned with trying to fix timetables. That is what Yeshua is warning us about here. We should avoid all "date guessing" prophecies. That leads to deception ("88 Reasons Why the Rapture Will Be in '88," the "Y2K bug" prophecies, etc.). However, that does not mean that we are not to be discerners of the times (see Mt. 16:3). He does not want us to be in the dark about the timing of end-time events (see 1 Thess. 5:4).

Restoring All Things

The Kingdom of God not only saves sinners from hell, but also restores the earth. When God created the earth in the beginning, He called it "very good." There was nothing wrong with the physical universe before the Fall. God is in the process of removing the sin of man and crushing the rebellion of Satan. When that work is completed, the earth will be restored.

Romans 8:20-21

For the creation was subjected to futility, not willingly, but because of Him who subjected it in hope;

Because the creation itself also will be delivered from the bondage of corruption into the glorious liberty of the children of God.

When men receive resurrection bodies, the earth will be renewed as well. There will be new heavens and a new earth, just as there were new heavens and a new earth after the flood of Noah. If there is no restoration of the earth, there is no need for bodily resurrection. As we believe in bodily resurrection, we also believe in the restoration of the earth.

In the biblical worldview, the land of Israel is seen as the first part of the earth to be restored. God made a covenant with the first believer (Abraham) to reclaim this portion of land. As the gospel spreads throughout the world, God makes a covenant with the true believers in each country to reclaim their land as well. Eventually all the earth will be reclaimed and restored.

From Heaven, Yeshua is directing the Church, Israel, and human society until God's will is fulfilled everywhere. Yeshua is in the process of restoring all good things through the Kingdom of God.

Acts 3:20-21

That He may send [Yeshua the Messiah], who was preached to you before,

Whom heaven must receive until the times of restoration of all things, which God has spoken by the mouth of all His holy prophets since the world began.

Eventually Yeshua will come back down out of Heaven, and all things will be restored. This perspective of restoration—that the Kingdom of God will remove all bad things from the earth and restore all good things—must be preached all around the world as part of the gospel before Yeshua can return (see Mt. 24:14).

This understanding of kingdom restoration is a prophetic message for the endtimes. It will be preached in the spirit of Elijah before the coming of the Messiah.

Matthew 17:11
Indeed Elijah is coming first and will restore all things.

When Yeshua comes again, He will sit on the throne of David and restore the kingdom to Israel. Yeshua was born and destined to reestablish the throne of David (see Chapter 12 of this book).

Luke 1:31-33
You will...bring forth a Son, and shall call his name [Yeshua]...

The Lord God will give Him the throne of His father David.

And He will reign over the house of Jacob forever, and of His kingdom there will be no end.

At that time a righteous and spiritual government will be restored to Israel. One of the daily prayers in traditional Judaism is for the reestablishment of righteous government in the land.

Isaiah 1:26
I will restore your judges as at the first, and your counselors as at the beginning. Afterward you shall be called the city of righteousness, the faithful city.

Notice the word *afterward*. There is a civil restoration within Israel first. Then comes the greater righteousness of the Kingdom of God. This description of the restoration of government in Israel in Isaiah 1 comes before the great vision of world peace in Isaiah 2. The restoration of righteous human government in Israel precedes the coming of the Messianic kingdom on earth.

If the earth is not to be restored, then there is no need for Israel to be restored. Yet if the earth is to be restored, so must the nation of Israel be restored. God made the first covenant with Abraham concerning the land of Israel. The restoration of Israel is the first part of the restoration of the world. The fact that the nation of Israel has already begun to be restored is a sign that we are coming closer to the second coming of Yeshua and to the restoration of all things.

CHAPTER 10

THE WORLD TRADE CENTER

In Israel, the first reaction to the September 11, 2001 attack on the World Trade Center was, "Why? Why didn't America listen to us all these years when we tried to warn them about the dangers of terrorism?"

The same spirit of terrorism that attacks Israel is also against America, and against evangelical Christians everywhere. The more that Christians see this connection, the better the defense against the attacks.

The second reaction in Israel was, "Where? Where were all the security and intelligence forces?" The fact that no one was ready for the attack indicates a great failure in United States defenses. Where were the FBI, the CIA, the NSA, the airline securities, etc.?

On further reflection, there was a great failure on our part, as Spirit-filled believers. Our prayers are supposed to be a spiritual security force. The attack therefore also pointed to a lack of effective intercessory prayer. Let us receive the September 11 attack as a wake-up call to a new level of spiritual warfare in these endtimes.

As I watched on television the destruction after the plane crashed into the first tower, I thought to myself, *What a huge victory this was for the terrorists*. But then as I saw the second plane crash unhindered into the second tower, I thought, *That is more than even the best terrorist can do*. There seemed to be a satanic empowerment, a kind of reverse "anointing." It was a supernatural attack of demonic forces as well.

Then we all watched both buildings collapse directly on top of themselves and disintegrate, without even falling sideways. I thought: *This is too much. Even the combined work of demonic forces and the best terrorists can't do that. An event of this magnitude has to reflect something of the hand of God as well.*

The mixture of those different influences (natural and supernatural; divine and demonic) makes it somewhat complicated to interpret what happened. Let's try to sort out some of the spiritual factors involved.

Not a Stone Upon a Stone

When Yeshua began His teaching on the endtimes, He started with a remark about the magnificent temple in Jerusalem.

Mark 13:2

Do you see these great buildings? Not one stone shall be left upon another, that shall not be thrown down.

Yeshua was not opposed to the temple. Quite the contrary, the temple was inspired and appointed by God to be the international center of worship. The temple represented the priestly calling of the Jewish people. However, any blessing can become a point of idolatry. When the people became more impressed with the grandeur of the temple than with simple faith and purity, the temple had to be destroyed.

God has blessed America with an almost unimaginable financial prosperity. The World Trade Center was exactly what its name implied—the center of international commerce. Its enormous buildings (stones) became the most recognizable symbol in the world of American financial prowess.

Unfortunately, many Americans have been more impressed with their blessings than with the God who gave them those blessings. Prosperity became the priority. Comfort replaced the cross. Entertainment replaced evangelism. Wealth became the religion, the WTC its temple.

The destruction of Jerusalem in A.D. 70 marked the end of an age. The destruction of the temple was the sign of that change. The destruction of the World Trade Center is a sign that we are passing into a new period of history. Spiritual warfare is intensifying. We are on the brink of end-times events, as described in the Book of Revelation.

The Glorified Woman

In the Book of Revelation, there are several symbolic images. One is the picture of a beautiful, glorified woman. This woman represents the people of God upon the earth. The Church is figuratively compared to a "bride" (see Eph. 5). The people of God are seen as getting ready to "marry" the Messiah.

Revelation 12:1

Now a great sign appeared in heaven: a woman clothed with the sun, with the moon under her feet, and on her head a garland of twelve stars.

This woman is pictured in Revelation 12 as engaged in a battle with the dragon, satan. In Revelation 19:6-10 she is described as having purified herself in holiness and good works. In Revelation 21 she is described as the heavenly city of Jerusalem descending to be joined with earthly Jerusalem below. Those three symbolic pictures represent three issues central to the community of faith in the endtimes: Spiritual warfare, personal purity, and identification with Jerusalem.

This beautiful maiden is described in Song of Solomon 6:13 as being made up of "two camps" or the "double camp." The two parts of this camp are Israel and the Church.

At this time these two camps are not united. The Church is mostly separated from her Jewish roots, and Israel is still mostly hardened to faith in Yeshua. However the trend of the endtimes will be for the two to grow more united. Yeshua's bride will be healed of her "schizophrenia" by the time He returns.

America is not the true Church, far from it. However, it is the country most identified with Christianity, and contains within it the strongest community of believers. The nation of Israel has not yet been restored to its spiritual destiny. However, it is in the process of being restored. The remnant within it is growing all the time.

While the two nations, America and Israel, are not the "Bride," they do represent that bride within the conflict of international politics and religion. Terrorist groups and militant Islamic clerics condemn America and Israel as "the big satan and the little satan." In that statement we can see a mirror image of the spiritual battle that is taking place.

Beauty and the Beast

Another major symbolic image in the Book of Revelation is a monster called the "Beast." The Beast is a political-military-religious conglomerate empowered by the devil. Its job is to attack the people of God. It encourages terrorist attacks against Christians and against Israelis.

Revelation 13:1b-2

I saw a beast rising up out of the sea, having seven heads and ten
horns, and on his horns ten crowns, and on his heads a blasphe-
mous name.

Now the beast which I saw was like a leopard, his feet were like
the feet of a bear, and his mouth like the mouth of a lion. The
dragon gave him his power, his throne, and great authority.

In the 1930s and '40s, the spirit of the beast was found mostly in
Nazism; in the 1950s through the '70s, mostly in communism. In our time,
it is found mostly in militant Islam—particularly when militant Islam has
the diplomatic backing of the United Nations.

In my opinion, the voice of the beast was heard at the United Nations
conference on racism in Durbin, South Africa, in August 2001. Radical Islamic groups at the conference marshaled an international coalition to condemn Israel. American and Israeli representatives walked out of the
meetings. The WTC attack followed soon after that conference.

In the 1991 Iraqi scud missile attacks on Israel, there was spontaneous
dancing in the streets in towns in the West Bank and other countries in the
Middle East. The same celebrations of dancing in the streets were also seen
in the first television coverage of the attack on the World Trade Center, even
though an effort was made to cover them up.

I am not saying that the Arab people are the beast. They are not the
beast any more than the Germans are because of Nazism, or the Russians
are because of communism, or the Jews are for having rejected Yeshua.
Arabs, Germans, Russians, Jews and all other humans are loved by God and
loved by those who are born of God (see 1 Jn. 4).

However, the great majority of the terrorist attacks in the world today
come from Islamic groups. Most of the persecution of Christian missionaries comes from Islamic groups. The spirit of the beast is being expressed in
our generation through terrorism, and that terrorism is being given religious
justification by extremist Islamic clerics.

Islam came into the world in the second half of the seventh century. In
some ways it was a reaction to the failure and corruption of both Judaism
and Christianity. If Judaism or Christianity were what they were supposed
to be, there never would have been such a void, which needed Islam to fill
it. Islam saw itself as the third stage, the better stage, after Judaism and

Christianity. Islam's conquest of the Middle East, and particularly of the holy places in Israel, was seen as divine proof of its supremacy over Judaism and Christianity.

Israeli journalist Nahum Barnea stated that the world today, since the fall of communism, is divided into three groups. The first world group is America, which rules in commerce, culture, and politics. The second world group is made up of those who are striving to become more like America. The third group is those who would like to see America's downfall. It is among that group that militant Islam has made the most gains.

The Bride and the Whore

Another symbolic image in the Book of Revelation is the harlot, or whore. The great whore is the spiritual counterfeit and perversion of the great bride. The whore goes wherever the bride is. The two spirits, one clean and one unclean, are found next to one another. The purpose of the spirit of the whore is to defile the bride (the community of true believers) internally, and then disqualify her in the eyes of the rest of the world.

Revelation 17:3b-4

I saw a woman sitting on a scarlet beast which was full of names of blasphemy, having seven heads and ten horns.

The woman was arrayed in purple and scarlet, and adorned with gold and precious stones and pearls, having in her hand a golden cup full of abominations and the filthiness of her fornication.

The whore is the spirit of lust, greed, and moral decadence. The scarlet color represents lust, the purple color represents religious hypocrisy, and the gold represents wealth. The description of this symbolic image is found throughout the Bible in pictures of the immoral woman (the Delilah figure in Judges 16, the adulterous woman in Proverbs 5–7, the woman of the curse in Zechariah 5, etc.). Wherever the true community of faith is found, there will also be counterfeit spirits of lust, greed, and moral decadence. Why is this so?

God desires to bless His people. One blessing is financial prosperity. Whichever country has the strongest community of faith eventually becomes the wealthiest. This wealth is not only to demonstrate God's covenant blessings, but also to finance world evangelism and to help the poor.

Another blessing to the community of faith is influence in culture and communication. Whichever culture has the strongest roots of faith will become the dominant world culture. Their language will become the dominant international language. When the early Church was strongest in Rome, Rome ruled the world, and their language became the world's language.

The third blessing is political power. This power is to help bring social justice and order to the world. These three blessings (financial prosperity, cultural influence, and political dominance) are meant for good. However, they also provide fertile ground for the sins of lust, greed, and moral decadence. This is why the whore is found in such close proximity to the bride.

America is not the Church nor is it the bride, but it does contain the strongest community of faith in our generation. English has become the international language. American culture influences the world. It is the strongest nation both financially and militarily.

America is not the great whore. However, the spirit of the whore is most found in America. Moral decadence in American society represents the great whore to the rest of the world. Scenes of lust and greed are projected all over the world through movies from Hollywood, advertising from Madison Avenue, and entertainment from cable television networks.

The spirit of the whore is found throughout Western society and very strongly in secular Israeli society. The moral decadence here is so bad that perhaps instead of saying, "the great satan and the little satan," we might call the worldliness in America and Israel "the big whore and the little whore."

America, as the dominant nation of the world, contains the greatest spirit of the bride and the greatest spirit of the whore. There is a constant struggle between purity and decadence. The same is true in Israel. In fact, that struggle between purity and carnality is found in every nation and in every person. The Holy Spirit influences him toward purity. The spirit of the world influences him toward carnality. Eve represents the bride when she is pure, the whore when she sins. Rahab (see Josh. 2) was a prostitute and Bat Sheba (see 2 Sam. 11) an adulteress, but then they both became part of the lineage of the Messiah (see Mt. 1). Israel in the Bible is called both the bride and the whore (see Hos. 2).

For those unbelievers around the world who are attracted to America, one wonders whether they are being attracted to the righteousness in America or to its decadence—to the bride or to the whore.

For those who are under the spirit of Islam, it is impossible to see the bride because of their different religious orientation. Therefore when they look at America, they see only the whore, not the bride. Radical Muslims see America as to blame for the moral decadence of the West. On this point they are partly correct, but they miss the underlying righteousness that also exists. The same is true when Palestinians look at Israel. They cannot see anything of the covenant promise on our people; they see only our sin and immorality.

Militant Muslims believe they have a divine mandate from Allah to rid the world of moral decadence. Since they see America and Israel as the sources of moral decadence, that mandate is translated into working to destroy those two nations. After the World Trade Center attack, Saddam Hussein remarked that it was Allah's punishment for America's decadence and for its support of Israel.

The Beast and the Whore

In the battle between America and Islamic terrorism, God has several spiritual purposes for the community of believers:

1.   To strengthen us to fight against the beast,
2.   To purify us from our whorishness,
3.   To use us for world evangelism,
4.   To draw Israel and the Church closer together.

At the same time, Satan is working to destroy, defile, and disfigure the community of faith all around the world. During this spiritual battle, God is able to take what the devil meant for evil and turn it to His purposes for good. While the dragon empowers the beast in order to kill the bride, God uses these attacks of the beast to purify the bride.

Revelation 17:16-17a

And the ten horns which you saw on the beast, these will hate the harlot, make her desolate and naked, eat her flesh and burn her with fire.

For God has put it into their hearts to fulfill His purpose.

This is an astonishing verse. The beast is demonic. So is the whore. Yet God uses one to destroy the other. God has allowed militant Muslim terrorists to so hate the moral decadence of the West that they are willing to attack. And so God uses this to His purposes. Although Islamic terrorism is completely demonic, it is also a tool in God's hand to bring judgment against Western decadence and to purge lust and carnality from the hearts of true believers.

The Judgment of God

In one and the same event, there is a demonic attack against the people of God and a judgment of God to purify His people. The purpose of endtimes judgments and disasters is to bring the people of the world to repentance.

Revelation 9:20-21
The rest of mankind, who were not killed by these plagues, did not repent of the works of their hands, that they should not worship demons, and idols of gold...

And they did not repent of their murders or their sorceries or their sexual immorality or their thefts.

Although most people in the world will not repent, some will. This idea is repeated again in Revelation 16:10-11. Just as God brought the plagues upon Egypt in the hope that some of them would repent, so will He bring judgments on the world in an effort to shake people out of their sinfulness. Most of the Egyptians did not repent, but some did (see Ex. 12:38). The plagues and judgments on Egypt were part of God's overall plan to redeem the people of Israel and bring glory to Himself. In the same way, the plagues and judgments of the endtimes are part of God's plan to bring world redemption and the Kingdom of God.

The WTC disaster caused many people to turn to God in repentance. Even heads of nations started praying. Christians around the world began identifying with Israel's battle against terrorism. Israel is starting to see itself as aligned with evangelical Christians. In the midst of all these disasters, the Kingdom of God is going forward.

The Fall of Babylon

The judgment of God on Western greed, decadence, and humanism is called "the fall of Babylon" (see Rev. 17–18). The whore of Babylon is seen as sitting upon many waters.

Revelation 17:1b,3b,15-16
Come, I will show you the judgment of the great harlot who sits on many waters.

I saw a woman sitting on a scarlet beast...

The waters which you saw, where the harlot sits, are peoples, multitudes, nations, and tongues.

And the ten horns which you saw on the beast, these will hate the harlot...

The many waters refer to multitudes of people. That the whore is "sitting" upon those multitudes refers to the worldly cultural influence over the nations. The third-world group of nations feel that they are being "sat upon" by the Western, primarily English-speaking world, which controls finances and the media. Those multitudes hate that dominance. Western moral decadence nurtures feelings of resentment in the rest of the world and thus gives grounds for the "hatred" of the beast spirit.

The World Trade Center was seen as the symbol of financial power, the White House as the symbol of political power, and the Pentagon as the symbol of military power. Therefore those three buildings were the targets of the September 11, 2001 attacks.

The whore of Babylon is referred to five times in Revelation 17–18 as "the great city." In Revelation 18:11 and 15, the whore of Babylon is pictured as the center for world trade, dealing with all the "merchants of the earth." It's not difficult to see an application of those two phrases to New York City and the World Trade Center.

There is also a veiled reference to a tower. The words "Babylon" and "Babel" in Hebrew are the same word—*bavel*. Therefore the fall of Babylon in Revelation 18 is identified with the tower of Babel in Genesis 11. Revelation 18:17 refers to the fall taking place in the space of "one hour." Again it's not difficult to see an application to the twin towers falling in the space of an hour or so.

Since the twin towers fell straight downward, the number of people injured was greatly limited, as compared to what might have happened had they fallen sideways. Even in the worst judgments of God, when demonic forces are temporarily released for attack, the hand of God is there to limit the destruction (see Rev. 9:4-5).

The fall of the World Trade Center was not the ultimate fall of Babylon described Revelation 17–18. However, it was an example of the spiritual warfare and divine judgment described there.

These two great evils, the whore and the beast, reflect two sides of evil within mankind. On the one side there is decadence, lust, and greed. On the other side there is violence, anger, and resentment. They are a left and right wing of the sinful nature of man. One side reflects the nature of satan as the tempter; the other side the nature of satan as the accuser.

The people of God find themselves attracted to the whore and attacked by the beast—caught between temptation and accusation. God wants to separate the bride from the whore and to protect the bride from the beast. We must have purity and humility on the one side, and faith and authority on the other side.

Revelation 18:4

I heard another voice from heaven saying, "Come out of her, my people, lest you share in her sins, and lest you receive of her plagues."

God calls His people to separate themselves from worldliness through repentance. He calls us to "come out" of the world. A wise man hears a word of reproof, while a fool needs to be beaten with a rod (see Prov. 10:13). If we cannot hear the message of repentance, judgment comes upon us. Part of God's method of judgment is to allow the beast spirit to attack the whore spirit. The lesson we need to learn is to get out of both.

Destruction of the Beast

God's purposes are not only to separate the bride from the whore, but also to destroy the beast. God will allow the beast to destroy the whore, and then He will destroy the beast. At the Second Coming, Yeshua Himself will destroy the beast. After that there will be left only the pure bride and King Messiah.

Revelation 17:14

These [the ten horns and kings of the beast] *will make war with the Lamb, and the Lamb will overcome them; for He is the Lord of lords and the King of kings.*

Yeshua will make war upon the beast in His role as King of kings. In a certain sense, President Bush, as the head of the strongest nation in the world, represents Yeshua's authority as King of kings. There is a parallel between Bush's desire to make war on terrorism with Yeshua's desire to make war with the beast.

We need to pray that the World Trade Center attack will mark the beginning of the destruction of terrorism and militant Islam. With the fall of communism in Russia, millions were exposed to the gospel. With the fall of Islam, millions will be exposed to the gospel as well.

Chapter 11

Terrorism and Propaganda

The September 11, 2001 attacks brought terrorism to a new level of awareness in the international community. In Israel, terrorism has been a day-to-day reality for many years. In response to the public disgust at terrorism, there has been an attempt by groups that supported terrorism to blur the meaning of what terrorism really is. For instance, there were accusations that Israeli settlements on the West Bank or American efforts to hunt down bin Laden were acts of terrorism.

Let us therefore try to arrive at a simple definition of just what terrorism is.

Terrorism: Acts of violence purposely targeted at innocent civilians for the purpose of gaining power or influence through widespread intimidation.

Terrorism is usually preceded by indoctrination in order to "demonize" the people who are about to be attacked, and to justify those who are making the attack. Terrorism is often done without official and formal backing of any government authority, even though a government may be supporting the terrorists behind the scenes. Let's analyze briefly the elements of this definition.

Purposeful Targeting

In Israel last year, more people were killed in car accidents than in terrorist acts. However, accidents are not purposefully planned, and, therefore, do not reflect an evil intention in the heart of the person who did it. There is grief at car accidents, but there is not a deep repulsion at the hideous evil that caused the act. It is the degree of hatred behind terrorism that makes it so horrible.

In one incident, five Palestinian children were killed when they kicked a discarded Israeli explosive. This horrible event brought an immediate apology by the Israeli government. An investigation showed that the army was negligent in leaving the explosive so close to a Palestinian school area. But no one who understands the Israeli mentality could entertain the thought that innocent children were purposely targeted. That event was a tragedy but not a terrorist attack.

Innocent Civilians

In the United States attacks against Al Qaida in Afghanistan, many civilians unfortunately were killed. Whenever United States forces operate, they must exercise restraint to keep the number of innocent civilian injuries as low as possible. If every possible effort is made to protect innocent civilians, military effort cannot be considered terrorism.

Baruch Goldstein's shooting of 29 innocent Arab Muslims at the mosque in Hebron in 1994 would be considered an act of terrorism. The Israeli government's hunting down and killing of the leaders of the Hamas and Jihad terrorist rings, who themselves are guilty of murder, could not be considered an act of terror.

To Gain Power or Influence

Terrorism usually has a political or religious goal. Bin Laden is after the destruction of Western society. Hamas and Hizbollah are out to destroy the Zionist enemy. That is terrorism. A jealous husband who kills his wife's supposed lover is guilty of murder, but not of terrorism—because no religious or political goal is sought. A husband's beating his wife to maintain control over her is quite similar to terrorism, but not technically the same.

The plane hijackings of the 1970s and '80s were designed to exert political pressure, a kind of public blackmail. Terrorism is sometimes committed by tyrants, such as Idi Amin or Saddam Hussein. In such cases, their goal is maintaining control over their country. The many instances of Islamic terrorism, and the few instances of orthodox Jewish terrorism, both involve religious indoctrination convincing the terrorist that he is achieving some greater goal concerning God's will. Yigal Amir's assassination of Yitzhak Rabin in 1995 was intended to destroy the peace movement as a whole in Israel.

Mass Intimidation

Terrorism is a kind of psychological warfare. The target of the terrorist attack is not so much the victims themselves, but the people who will hear about the event. Terrorism, therefore, is much enhanced by modern mass media. It is almost impossible to have terrorism without the accompanying propaganda or publicity.

The power of terrorism is its ability to create fear in a large number of people. It spreads intimidation through mass psychology. Therefore, terrorist attacks are often accompanied by video or radio broadcasts with exaggerated claims of destruction. Those claims may have little connection to the actual capability of the group, but the intimidating words are part of the terrorism.

Illegal Authority

Terrorist groups usually start without any constitutional or elected basis of authority. The terrorism is to gain power and influence through illegal means. After a reign of terror, these groups are often able to gain enough support to be elected. Hitler started with terrorism and eventually was elected. The same was true of Stalin. Arafat started as a terrorist without governmental authority, but then was elected as chairman of the Palestinian Authority.

With an unauthorized group, it is difficult to hold someone accountable. Whom do you punish? Whom do you attack? Who will take responsibility for maintaining law and order? The Syrian government, although it supports Hizbollah, claims that it is not responsible for its actions. The Palestinian Authority maintains that it is not responsible for the terrorist acts of Hamas and Jihad.

Part of this syndrome is that the terrorists are usually experts at vengeance and intimidation, but have little ability or willingness to build a constructive and responsible solution. It's easier to burn down a house than to build one.

Indoctrination

Since human beings have a certain degree of God-given moral conscience, terrorist acts would be naturally abhorrent to the normal person. Therefore, brainwashing must take place to prepare the ground for the terrorist to reverse his moral human instinct. Timothy McVeigh was indoctrinated in libertarian extremism. The Germans were brainwashed with the notion that the Aryan race was superior. Stalin was able to seize power by exploiting Marxist-Leninist propaganda. Yigal Amir was brainwashed by ultra-orthodox rabbinic teachings and by right-wing political extremism. Today millions of Muslims have been indoctrinated to believe that Jews are evil, that Palestine is holy land to Islam, and that America and Israel are manifestations of satan.

Political or religious indoctrination is part of the terrorist process. This brainwashing creates a "demonized" image of the people who are potential victims, and a heroic image of the terrorist himself. Thus, he justifies his own act of murder and glorifies himself in the eyes of his friends. Hamas and Jihad raise money to support the families of suicide terrorists, so that the terrorist can feel he is doing a heroic act to help his destitute family members.

Isaiah 5:20a
Woe to those who call evil good and good evil.

One of the most difficult challenges of peace efforts in Israel is the indoctrination of the Palestinian children at a very young age to see all Israelis as monsters and to glorify suicide terrorism as a "holy" action. One aspect of this brainwashing is the promise that every suicide terrorist will receive an immediate entrance to the Garden of Eden and 70 beautiful virgins to serve him sexually for eternity.

In one instance two young Palestinians attempted a suicide bombing. Something went wrong with the bombs, and they both survived. They were taken unconscious to Israeli Secret Service for interrogation. The interrogators were surprised to find that the young men had sprayed perfume on themselves and wrapped their male organs with protective bandages. (A cynical joke went around Israel that when the young men finally awoke in the cement-walled basement of Israeli General Security headquarters, the grim interrogator's first words to them were, "This isn't the Garden of Eden, and I'm no virgin.")

Recently, there have even been some attempts at terrorist attacks by children as young as age ten. Some of them do this with the blessing of their parents, some without. In one instance, a twelve-year-old child was picked up by Palestinian police on his way to perform a terrorist attack. He told the police chief that he was hoping to go to paradise and receive his 70 virgins. The chief reportedly asked him, "Do you know what a virgin is?" The young boy simply answered, "No."

Islamic brainwashing of Palestinian children toward suicide martyrdom is not humorous. It is tragic beyond words.

Propaganda and Media Distortion

Not only must there be brainwashing of the terrorists themselves, there must also be a concerted media campaign to make the terrorism effective. That propaganda has several aspects. First, there is the objective to exaggerate the power of the terrorist group. The stronger their image, regardless of their actual resources, the more intimidation they can project.

Secondly, they want the gory details of the terrorist attack to be well publicized. Pictures of blood and body parts repeated again and again on television can make even a small attack inflict fear on millions.

Thirdly, they want to picture themselves not as terrorists but as freedom fighters. Much propaganda goes toward developing this image. The liberal media is usually quite cooperative in portraying the terrorists in that role. They want to be negotiated with as diplomats instead of as terrorists.

Fourthly, as mentioned above, the targets of the terrorist attacks must be portrayed as monsters. To justify the terrorism, lies are told about atrocities committed by the enemy. A new edition of the spurious book *Elders of Zion*, in Arabic, is being spread throughout the Middle East. This book portrays the ridiculous myth that there are secret meetings of Jewish leaders who are planning to take over the world. The book was written in Russian over one hundred years ago. It was used by Hitler to encourage anti-Semitism. Although the book is a complete lie, it is presented as if it were a history text.

Fifthly, the terrorists want to blur the meaning of terrorism so they will not be accused of terrorism. Every one else is guilty of terrorism in their eyes; therefore they are not guilty. They constantly accuse their targets (particularly Americans and Israelis) of being terrorists, thereby justifying their own actions. Unfortunately, the media often repeat these distortions to the point that they begin to seem reasonable to many people.

This media distortion has been a major problem for Israel. I would like to give one example to illustrate the point. In early 2002, a terrorist cell in Jenin hit Israel with a series of terrorist attacks. This group was the most dangerous and developed terrorist cell in the territories.

The Israeli army called up a reserve unit, mostly of middle-aged dads, to go in and clear out the cell. For months there was a propaganda campaign accusing Israel of mass murder. The media repeated the claim that over five hundred were brutally killed. That claim was so well publicized that it was received as a proven fact all over the world. A few months later, when the investigation showed that fewer than 50 people were killed in two weeks of hand-to-hand fighting, the damage had already been done.

Interviews With Israeli Soldiers at Jenin

Here are some eyewitness accounts of the fighting that took place in Jenin. These excerpts were taken from a series of interviews by Moshe Ronen, reporter for the *Yidiot Aharonot* newspaper in Israel.

Shlomi Leniado, age 33, from Hod HaSharon, married with 2 children, director of a theater production group:

"Our unit was being shot at—and it was forbidden for us to shoot back without permission because there were civilians in the camp. We were permitted only to shoot when there was a clear target and that target was a terrorist who was shooting at us. We felt as if we were being shot at from all sides but we could not shoot back unless we had a clearly identified target. Because of this, we were wounded. And there were those of us who were getting killed—because we have a heart. We paid a price with our lives because of our moral values.

"When we got to the United NationsWRA building (United Nations World Relief Agency), we were shot at by armed men from within. When we got inside, we found no evidence of any humanitarian activity.

"One day next to the Kalandiah barrier, we caught an ambulance from the Red Crescent which was transporting explosives." [You see the obvious moral dilemma.]

Dr. David Tsangan, a pediatrician, head of the children's endocrinology unit at Hadassah Hospital in Jerusalem and father of 4:

"As the medic of our division, I was involved in all the medical treatments and was aware of every detail of the operation in Jenin. I cannot help but be deeply stirred by the high moral integrity of the soldiers in the IDF. The fighting there was, without exception, only against the terrorists.

"The place was not a refugee camp but an armed and booby-trapped fortress, within which were entrenched 200 terrorist fighters, whose only goal there was to enlist new boy and girl terrorists from the ages of 16 to 20. We searched from house to house, and we found photographs of these teenage boys and girls strapped with explosive belts. These boy and girl suicide terrorists had not yet committed suicide but were already photographed as being ready.

"I am a pediatrician who treats many Arab children. At Hadassah Hospital in Jerusalem, about half of our patients are Arabs. They arrive from Shechem, from Hebron, from Bethlehem, and from Jenin. As a pediatrician, it was difficult for me to see those photographs of young future suicide terrorists.

"In this terrorist fortress [the Jenin refugee camp], we found very few normal citizens. Some of the citizens were collaborators with the terrorists, while others were hostages in their hands. The terrorists hid behind the citizens and in their houses. We could have used artillery or planes to bomb the houses, but we did not do so. In several instances, our soldiers were wounded, because we were forbidden to detonate the houses for fear that there might be women or children in them.

"They made use of children for the most horrible things. We met there a child around 6 years old who was carrying a bag. When the soldiers asked him what was in the bag, he threw it toward them and ran. Inside the bag were found three pipe bombs.

"In one of their ambulances we found a young man being transported who was supposedly in critical condition. We checked him and found out that he was a wanted terrorist, who was completely healthy. He didn't have a scratch on him. The IV that was supposedly attached to him was just stuck to his shirtsleeve with a band-aid."

Yehuda Mashav, 30, an accountant, married, from Tel Aviv:

"We went from house to house. When we found civilians in a house we concentrated them into one of the rooms and made a search through the house to see if there were explosives or wanted terrorists hiding there. We tried to help the civilians get through that traumatic experience in peace. To those who didn't have any food, we gave them of our own food.

"Every few meters that we advanced forward, we stopped and asked for the civilians to get out of the houses in order not to endanger anyone. Those who turned themselves over to us, primarily women and children, received from us chocolates, candy and mineral water, which we gave them out of our own rations. We simply had compassion upon them.

"In order to prevent innocent civilians from being wounded, we were left exposed, and were wounded ourselves. Thirteen of our soldiers were killed in one day; they were hit because we wanted to prevent any bombing from the air."

Itamar Gamliel, 27, security director, computer company *Amdox*, Herzilya:

"There was a battle over every house. There was not even one house that we entered without a fight. Half of the camp was emptied, booby-trapped with explosives, and there were snipers in every window.

"For such fighting were needed great patience, responsibility and caution. These reservists had just those qualities. I was filled with awe at my fellow soldiers in the IDF. We did the job in the highest level of moral standards. Our losses were caused only for that reason. Our orders were only to shoot on verified sources of fire. We risked our lives because of that den of wasps. The camp was crowded—one house on top of another. They were shooting at us from everywhere, and we were prevented from returning fire whenever there was a fear of wounding some civilians."

Avishai Baviyof, 38, a businessman from Yavne, married and father of 3:

"All the accusations about a slaughter that supposedly happened in the Jenin refugee camp are all 100% lies and nonsense. We did not hurt even one civilian intentionally. They are simply waging a propaganda war. They were using women and children as a defensive line—and after that they claimed that we injured women and children. How cynical can you get? I have three children, and I very much want to get home."

Media Distortion and Propaganda War

As part of the analysis of the media distortion that took place over the Jenin battle, I would like to include as well excerpts from an article by Jerome Marcus, which appeared in the *Wall Street Journal* on April 30, 2002. Again, my point is simply to emphasize that terrorism goes hand in hand with propaganda. The terrorism needs propaganda, and the propaganda needs the media. Terrorism is essentially a propaganda war:

"The United Nations is intent on investigating charges that Israeli forces violated the human rights of Palestinians during this month's raid on the Jenin refugee camp. Because noncombatants were killed there, the word 'massacre' is being bandied about in the press. Many in the 'human rights community' have already reached a verdict.

"In Article 58 of its Protocol relating to the Protection of Victims of International Armed Conflicts, the Geneva Convention says those in control of territory must 'endeavor to remove the civilian population, individual civilians and civilian objects under their control from the vicinity of military objectives; Avoid locating military objectives within or near densely populated areas; Take the other necessary precautions to protect the civilian population.'

"George H. Aldrich, the chief American negotiator of this treaty, has explained that under it, 'a party in control of territory is instructed to take all feasible measures to protect civilians and civilian objects from the effects of combat, largely by trying to separate them to the extent possible from military objectives.' Such a party must therefore 'avoid unnecessarily sighting military objectives near civilian dwellings.'

"The Palestinian terrorists did the exact opposite. Rather than 'avoid unnecessarily sighting military objectives near civilian dwellings,' they hid such 'objectives' almost exclusively in dwellings and other civilian buildings: The bomb factories Israel found throughout the West Bank were located in homes, schools and other civilian sites. And rather than 'trying to separate, to the extent possible, from military objectives,' the terrorists went out of their way to hide military objectives behind, in, around and under civilian (and even humanitarian) objectives. The ambulance containing the bomb belt; the pregnant young woman in 'labor' who turns out to be about to give birth to a bomb—these are the most explicit possible violations of the international human rights of the population in whose midst these military objectives are hidden.

"In a post-battle interview with the Cairo weekly *Al-Ahram*, an Arab bomb maker named 'Omar' proudly laid out the Palestinians' strategy of militarizing homes: 'We had more than 50 houses booby-trapped around the camp,' he said. Unarmed women lured Israeli soldiers to their deaths.

"The Palestinian terrorists used the civilian population like this, we know, because that is part of their strategy: make victims and then cry about victims. Plus, knowing they cannot face the IDF in the field, the terrorists tried to cripple the Israeli army by hiding among civilians, thereby forcing the real soldiers to hold back. The Palestinians knew that the Israelis—a disciplined army of husbands and fathers—would restrain themselves to avoid killing noncombatants.

"Even Arab fighters have admitted the Israelis did exactly that. Captured Jenin-based terrorist Thabet Mardawi told CNN last week that he 'and other Palestinian fighters had expected Israel to attack with planes and tanks.' 'I couldn't believe it when I saw the soldiers,' he said. 'The Israelis knew that any soldier who went into the camp like that was going to get killed.' Shooting at these men as they walked cautiously down the street 'was like hunting….like being given a prize….I've been waiting for a moment like that for years.'

"Can it be any clearer? The 13 Israeli soldiers killed in that Jenin deathtrap died precisely because they were trying to discriminate between military and nonmilitary 'objectives' the way a Daisy Cutter can't. In other words, they were trying to undo the effect of the human rights violations inflicted on the population of Jenin by the terrorist army that made its home there.

"Eventually, of course—as was certain to happen so long as they were not pulled out too soon—the Israelis were successful in their mission. But the Palestinian terrorists, having planted themselves among civilians, have harvested a fresh crop of victims, which they are now using for public-relations purposes. The United Nations investigation in Jenin is the fruit of that PR campaign. What the terrorists did to harvest that fruit, however, is the real violation of the West Bank residents' human rights."

Reconciliation

We as believers in Yeshua must have an answer to terrorism and propaganda. That answer is reconciliation. We have not only been reconciled to God through the gospel of Jesus (see 2 Cor. 5:19), we have also been reconciled to one another.

Ephesians 2:14
For He Himself is our peace, who has made both one, and has broken down the middle wall of separation.

An essential aspect of the Kingdom of God here in Israel is the testimony of reconciliation between Israeli Messianic Jews and Palestinian Christians. We do truly love one another. Often there is stress between us because of the difficulty of the political situation. Yet by faith we have to continue to overcome our differences, to forgive one another as Yeshua forgave us, and let the cross of Yeshua be more important to us than any political issue. Our reconciliation is a powerful testimony of the grace of God in our midst. Please pray for this important testimony to be strengthened and to grow.

CHAPTER 12

THE THRONE OF DAVID

Christ, of course, is not Jesus' last name; it is His title. *Christ* means "christened one" or "anointed one." The word in Hebrew is *Mashiach* from which we get the English word "Messiah." Jesus is the Christ, the Messiah, the anointed one.

Prophet, Priest, and King

Three types of people were anointed in the Old Testament. One was the priest who performed the ritual sacrifices (see Ex. 29:7; 30:30; Lev. 16:32). The second was the king (see 1 Sam. 15:1; 2 Sam. 2:4; 1 Kings 1:39). The third kind was the prophet (see 1 Kings 19:16; Isaiah 61:1).

This anointing symbolized the power of the Holy Spirit to enable the person to fulfill his office as prophet, priest, or king. Yeshua, as the Messiah, fulfills all three of those offices at the highest level. Very few other men who were able to be anointed in all three offices. Moses was one of them, and perhaps Ezra. David and Joshua were kings and prophets, but not priests. Ezekiel and Jeremiah were priests and prophets, but not kings.

When ancient Israel was in a godly condition, those three anointed offices came closer together. If the nation was in a sinful condition, there was division between those offices. As the nation grew even more sinful, it had to be totally divided in half. The northern kingdom had its own kings and prophets, although no priests. The priesthood was confined only to the tribe of Levi with its center in Judea. In other words, the prophet and king positions were transferable to other tribes, but the priesthood was connected only to Levi and Judah.

When Israel reached its worse spiritual condition, it was scattered among the nations. The first exile was to Babylon in 586 B.C. The second and greater exile started in A.D. 70 and continued until 1948 with the founding of the state of Israel. The first exile was a little more than 70 years; the second exile was almost 2,000 years.

While Yeshua is the Messiah, other men have filled the offices of prophet, priest, or king in their generation. Each prophet, priest, or king was considered to be a messiah, an anointed minister, serving in his ordained office.

When Israel rejected the Messiah, the offices of prophet and king were taken away and given to the gentile nations. Rabbinic Judaism, in its traditions, preserved the symbols of the ancient temple priests. Since the temple was destroyed as part of the punishment, they cannot function in that office, but the traditions have at least preserved the rituals of the priesthood.

The Spirit of Prophecy

The spirit of prophecy was received by the disciples of Yeshua on the day of Pentecost (Shavuot). It was then transferred from them to other believers in all the nations of the world. In a certain sense, all Spirit-filled, born-again believers in Yeshua carry with them the prophetic anointing. The gospel is the continuation of the spirit of prophecy and the message of the prophets. "For the testimony of Jesus is the spirit of prophecy" (Rev. 19:10).

Therefore, the true Church (the universal community of faith in Yeshua) is a prophetic body. It is neither governmental (kingly), nor religious (priestly). All of the offices of authority within the body of believers (apostles, prophets, evangelists, pastors, and teachers) are spiritual in nature. They all have a type of prophetic anointing.

In that sense, the separation of church and state is correct. Just being a pastor does not mean that someone has direct constitutional authority over the government. Prophetic anointing gives a spiritual authority over the government in prayer and preaching (see Jer. 1:10), but it does not give legislative authority or executive office. A Spirit-filled believer may enter the political realm, but he does so on the merits and qualifications of being able to govern, and not simply because he is a believer.

Separation of church and state is also correct in the sense that a political leader should not be able to legislate which religion the citizens must join. Nor is it correct for a certain denominational leader to be given the authority to appoint the head of the government. When Yeshua returns, those three offices will be joined together again in Him.

Christianity is not meant primarily to be a religion. Yeshua did not come to bring a new religion, but to give us forgiveness of sins and eternal life. There is enough religion in the Old Testament. There is only one religion in the Bible; it is Judaism. The Church is a prophetic body. Since the Jewish priesthood is currently in rebellion to Yeshua, part of the priestly functions had to be transferred to the Church.

The Government Anointing

As the prophetic anointing was transferred to the international Spirit-filled community of faith, so was the kingly anointing passed on to whatever nation was allowed by God to have the greatest ability to govern. At the beginning of the first exile, the kingly anointing was given to Nebuchadnezzar (see Jer. 27:6). At the end of the first exile, it was given to Cyrus. In fact, Cyrus is referred to as the Messiah: "Thus says the Lord to His anointed [messiah], to Cyrus...to subdue nations before him" (Is. 45:1).

At the time of Yeshua, the kingly office was in the hands of the Roman Empire. Yeshua freely admitted to Pilate that his Father in Heaven had granted to Pilate the governmental authority to crucify Him (see Jn. 19:11). The priests, on the other hand, did not have that governmental authority. That is why they went to Pilate to ask him to put Yeshua to death (see Jn. 18:31). At the Crucifixion, those Jews in the priestly office asked Pilate, in the kingly office, to crucify Yeshua, who was at the time operating in His prophetic office.

In our generation, the kingly authority is in the hands of the United States. In the previous century, it was in the hands of the British Empire. In each generation, there is one man ordained by God, who serves as the head of all governmental authority on earth. At this time that office is the president of the United States. He does not have the prophetic or priestly office, but the government is in his hands.

Jeremiah 27:6-9

I have given all these lands into the hand of Nebuchadnezzar, the King of Babylon, My servant...

So all nations shall serve him...until the time of his land comes...

And it shall be, that the nation and kingdom which will not serve Nebuchadnezzar the King of Babylon...that nation I will punish...

Do not listen to your prophets...who speak to you, saying, "You shall not serve the King of Babylon."

Since the rebirth of the nation of Israel in 1948, and the renewed office of the prime minister, there has been a restoration of the kingly office within Israel. The prime minister is the equivalent of the ancient king of Israel. The highest official in every nation is the "king" of that nation.

The chief rabbis in Israel serve in a partial sense in the office of the priesthood. That is what Yeshua meant when He said: "The scribes and the Pharisees sit in Moses' seat" (Mt. 23:2. He was not referring to a kingly or prophetic office, but to their right to govern the temple rituals.

The Throne of David

When Yeshua returns, He will take up His place as both king of Israel and King of kings. Since the United States is the highest governing authority in the world today, the president of the United States serves as both the king of the United States and the king of kings. When Yeshua returns, Israel will become the most powerful nation of the world, and therefore Yeshua, as the head of the government of Israel, will be both the king of Israel and the King of kings.

Today the president of the United States sits in Yeshua's office as the king of kings, and the prime minister of Israel sits in Yeshua's office as the king of Israel. One day, those two positions will be united into one.

The prime minister's position in Israel is the renewal of the throne of David, which will ultimately be occupied by Yeshua. The first person to hold that position in modern times was David Ben Gurion. Because of the spiritual significance of that office there is an intense, almost intoxicating, fascination with Israeli elections and politics.

It is important to pray for God's will to be done in the government of Israel. The make-up of the Israeli government has spiritual significance for the purposes of God's kingdom throughout the world. The idea that the prime minister of Israel's office leads to the coming of the Messiah is a concept foreign to most of the Christian world, yet it is quite biblical. Not only is it biblical, but it is well known in the orthodox Jewish world. One of the 18 traditional benedictions that have been prayed every day for two thousand years is "Kisei David," for the reestablishment of the throne of David.

Interestingly enough, this benediction is prayed right before the benediction of the coming of the Messiah. This is logical. First, the government structure of King David is established; then the Messiah, son of David, will come to occupy it. Both the reestablishment of the structure for the Messiah's government, and the desire in the hearts of the people for the Messiah to come, must precede the coming of the Messiah. Here is the order: reestablishment, then revival, then return.

In the international community of faith, that first step of reestablishment is not needed. Why? First, because the gentile nations have not been exiled from their lands as punishment. Secondly, the promise of the earthly governing authority of Yeshua was given to David's seed. Therefore, the restoration of government to other nations is not part of the prerequisites of the coming of the Messiah, as it is to Israel.

For the other nations, the order is simply two steps: revival, then return. The gospel must be preached to the nations (see Mt. 24:14); they must cry out, "Maranatha, come, Lord Jesus" (see Rev. 22:20); and then He returns. However, for Israel, the requirements for the return of Yeshua include this other step of the restoration of David's throne.

Of the Increase of His Kingdom

God made a covenant with David that his seed would be the Messiah and ruler of the world.

2 Samuel 7:12b-14,16

I will set up your seed after you, who will come from your body, and I will establish his kingdom.

He shall build a house for My name, and I will establish the throne of his kingdom forever.

I will be his Father, and he shall be My son.

And your house and your kingdom shall be established forever...

This promise is repeated throughout the Old Testament in many forms (see 1 Chron. 17; Psalm 89, etc.).

What astonished David about this promise was the word *forever* (see 2 Sam. 7:25). He did not understand how, but he noticed that the kingdom would include eternal life. One of the jobs of the Messiah is not just to sit on David's throne, but to bring eternal life to the people. What good would it be to God to establish His kingdom if His people were to die? For that reason, none of David's regular sons could fulfill the promises of the kingdom.

So God took David's kingdom and expanded it from the dimension of time into eternity. Then, to the prophet Isaiah, God promised to expand it in terms of population to all the nations of the world. How could God have a kingdom if it were not open to all the humans He had created? That is why we preach the gospel to all nations.

Isaiah 2:2

...and all nations shall flow to it.

Isaiah 56:7

...My house shall be called a house of prayer for all nations.

So God's plan was to take the kingdom of David and expand it two ways: By the dimension of time—eternally, and by the dimension of population—internationally. And the person through whom God would expand and establish the kingdom is none other than David's greater son, the Messiah.

Isaiah 9:7

Of the increase of His government and peace there will be no end, upon the throne of David and over His kingdom, to order it and establish it with judgment and justice from that time forward, even forever.

It would be the job of the Messiah to increase David's kingdom, not to do away with it. He would come to establish David's government, not to destroy it. He would come to sit on David's throne, not to remove it. Yeshua was born to fulfill God's covenant promises to David.

Luke 1:32-33

He will be great, and will be called the Son of the Highest; and the Lord God will give Him the throne of His father David.

And He will reign over the house of Jacob forever, and of His kingdom there will be no end.

Yeshua was resurrected from the dead to give us the eternal life that God promised to David. The gospel is an invitation to all nations to join the Messianic kingdom. After all nations are given a chance to receive eternal life, Yeshua will return to establish David's kingdom on the earth.

King of the Jews

Not only was Yeshua born to be King of the Jews, He was also crucified to be King of the Jews.

Matthew 27:11,29,37,42

...And the governor asked [Jesus], *saying, "Are You the King of the Jews?" Jesus said to him, "It is as you say."*

...And they bowed the knee before Him and mocked Him, saying, "Hail, King of the Jews!"

...And they put up over His head the accusation written against Him: This is Jesus the King of the Jews.

...If He is the King of Israel, let Him now come down from the cross, and we will believe Him.

Yeshua was crucified not only to give us forgiveness of sins, but also to establish His right to be the King of the Jews. On the cross, He purchased salvation for our sakes. But He also purchased something for Himself. On the cross, He purchased kingdom authority. So when we preach the gospel, we have two motivations: One for the human race, the other for Yeshua. For the people, we seek to save them from hell; for Yeshua, we seek to establish His kingdom. First we make Him King in our own lives. Then we seek to establish Him as King in the rest of the world.

Proverbs 14:28a

In a multitude of people is a king's honor.

Having people saved helps to establish Yeshua's kingdom. He wouldn't want a kingdom with hardly any people in it.

In addition, Yeshua was crucified to prove His moral right to sit on David's throne. The Cross was a test of obedience. Since He passed the test, He was given authority (see Phil. 2:7). Our ministry is not just for human beings. We are doing something for Yeshua. Our goal is to get Yeshua back into the earth to fulfill His destiny as King of the Jews. We want to help Him to accomplish what He died on the cross to do.

The Roof of the Temple

There was a discussion among the rabbis as to how the temple described in Ezekiel 40–42 would be built. On the one hand, there were specific instructions to build it. On the other hand, the whole project seemed supernatural. Some rabbis said that the people would build the temple. Others thought that the temple would descend completely from the sky. They compromised on the decision: We Jews would build the floors and the walls, and then God would make the roof descend from the heavens.

While the conclusion is not true, there is a point here. The Kingdom of God is not built completely by us. Nor does it descend completely from Heaven. We have a part to play, and then God completes it. This is why we preach the gospel, cast out demons, heal the sick, give money to the poor, and raise up leadership in the body of believers. We do as much as we can to bring the kingdom, and then God finishes it.

This is also why we are involved in the reestablishment of David's throne. The government of Israel is certainly not the Kingdom of God. On the other hand, the restoration of the state of Israel is part of the process that leads up to the coming of Yeshua and the establishment of His kingdom on earth. He is coming to take up a throne. Yes, He will add to it eternal life, world peace, and many other glorious things. However, there must be the foundation of a government structure here for Him to take up.

Two Thrones

Since Yeshua is both the Son of God and the son of David, He has two thrones: One in heaven and one on the earth. The one on earth was at one time Solomon's glorified throne (see 1 Kings 10). During modern history, it has been divided up into the offices of the heads of government of the nations of the world. Yet there is also a throne in the sky:

Ezekiel 1:26

Above the firmament over their heads was the likeness of a throne, in appearance like a sapphire stone; on the likeness of the throne was a likeness with the appearance of a man...

Ezekiel's vision is a picture of Yeshua and His throne in Heaven. But one day, that throne in Heaven will become one with the throne on earth (see Is. 6). Yeshua's authority, both in Heaven and on earth, will be united (see Eph. 1:10; Mt. 28:18). The physical comes first, then the spiritual. God first created physical man, then He gave us the new birth (see 1 Cor. 15:46-47). God will restore a basic structure of government in Israel, then Yeshua will return.

Crowning David King

The story of David's kingdom in the Bible teaches us some spiritual principles about the establishment of Yeshua's kingdom. First came Saul's kingdom, then David's. David was anointed as king long before he took up his position as king. Yeshua was anointed as king at the beginning of His ministry, but He has yet to take up His throne on earth.

Right before David became king, he was invited by the tribes of Israel and by the tribe of Judah. Likewise, before Yeshua's return to earth, He will be invited by the international Church (symbolized by the northern tribes of Israel) and by the Messianic Jewish remnant (symbolized by the tribe of Judah).

When David was old, there was a competition between two of his sons to become king in his place (see 1 Kings 1): One king was false (Adonijah); the other king was true (Solomon). Each one had their supporters, their prophets, and their priests. However, one was of God, and the other not. So it is today that there will be many false messiahs, but only one is real.

This involves a concept from the Old Testament called *hamlacha*. There is no word for it in English, but it means "to make someone king" or "to crown someone as king." David was previously anointed and appointed to be king by God. However, he did not come into his role as king of Israel until there was a core of leaders who were ready to inaugurate him. His servants had worked many years to establish his kingdom.

In Israel there was a long campaign by the followers of the Lubavitcher Rebbe to declare him to be the messiah, and thus, in effect, make him the messiah. They said he was already the messiah potentially, and if the people of Israel would make him king (hamlacha), then he would become the messiah in action. [Here I am describing some concepts that unfortunately are difficult to express in English, but come across much simpler in Hebrew.]

David waited until the elders of Judah—those with human authority over the government of Israel—were ready to declare him as king.

2 Samuel 5:3

All the elders of Israel came to the king at Hebron, and King David made a covenant with them at Hebron before the Lord. And they anointed David king over Israel.

This is what Yeshua referred to when He said that He would not return until the people of Jerusalem were ready to declare Him as king.

Matthew 23:39

You shall see Me no more till you say, "Blessed is He who comes in the name of the Lord!"

The idea that this blessing is connected with "king-making" is also seen in Mark's version of the triumphal entry.

Mark 11:9b-10a

Blessed is He who comes in the name of the Lord!

Blessed is the kingdom of our father David that comes in the name of the Lord!

This is more than just an invitation; it is an inauguration. It is a declaration of coronation, of kingship, of *hamlacha*. This is a reversal of what the people cried out in the courtyard over Yeshua (see Mt. 27:22). One day, instead of shouting, "Crucify Him!" our people will cry out, "Crown Him!"

Here are the last words of Yeshua:

Revelation 22:16b,20

I am the root and the offspring of David...

Surely I am coming quickly.

Yeshua was born as the son of David, He died on the cross as the son of David, and He is coming back as the son of David to take up His throne.

CHAPTER 13

OF TRUMPETS AND TRIBULATIONS

Most Israelis miss the significance of the 9-11 date of the twin towers disaster, not knowing that in the United States, 911 is the national telephone code to dial for emergency rescue help. What non-Israelis might miss is the connection of this September date to the "Feast of Trumpets" (see Lev. 23).

This connection is blurred by the fact that the biblical calendar is on a lunar basis, while the international calendar is solar. (In other words, the Feast of Trumpets falls on slightly different dates each year—although generally in the second week of September.) It is also blurred by the fact that the rabbis changed the name of the holy day from the "Feast of Trumpets," as it is in the Bible, to *Rosh Hashanah* or the Jewish *New Year.*

It was one year before the 9-11 disaster in New York that Ariel Sharon visited the Temple Mount, which caused such a huge outbreak of terrorism and conflict in the Middle East. Sharon's visit was connected with the Feast of Trumpets in the sense that he used the timing of the traditional holy day as an opportunity to express his identification with the Temple Mount.

That "trumpet" event in the year 2000 turned the Middle East upside down. In 2001 the 9-11 disaster turned the rest of the world upside down. The local disaster here in Israel preceded the international one. The conflicts that start here will always later reach the rest of the world. (Compare First Peter 4:17.)

In Leviticus 23, the Jewish people are commanded to blow the trumpet on the Feast of Trumpets, but there is no further explanation. In Revelation chapters 8–11 we find seven "trumpets" heralding huge disastrous events that precede the second coming of Yeshua. Although most Jews and Christians do not see the connection, the Feast of Trumpets and the seven trumpet judgments are connected one to another.

Actually, the word in Hebrew for the Feast of Trumpets is *Yom Teruah*. The word here is not "trumpet" but rather "blowing." The word *Teruah* has a double meaning—not only "blowing a trumpet," but also "alarm" or "warning." The thought is one of "sound the alarm" or "give an advance warning" or "call the people to alert." The emphasis is not on the ritual of blowing the shofar, but on the message of warning the people before an imminent catastrophe.

These earth-shaking events—the Feast of Trumpets and the seven trumpets of Revelation—serve as warnings to call people to turn to God before the coming of the Messiah. The fall of the New York towers was an historic, earth-shaking event. Yet that will seem small compared to the final seven trumpet events described in the Book of Revelation.

The blowing of the shofar is a priestly act by the religious Jewish community. The preaching of the Kingdom of God comes from the prophetic anointing of the Spirit-filled believers in Yeshua. The end-times events that will shake the nations of the world point to the authority of Yeshua as the soon-coming King. The three together express the image of priest, prophet, and king found in Messiah Yeshua.

The Day of Atonement is considered the greatest day of the priestly calendar, according to the Law of Moses. The greatest day in the eyes of the Hebrew prophets was "the great and awesome day of the Lord" (Joel 2:31). The greatest day of New Testament prophecy is the second coming of Yeshua. They're all the same day—The Day. The Torah, the Prophets, and the Messiah all agree.

Appointed Times

The Hebrew word for "feast" or "holy day" in the Bible is *mo'ed*. It is better translated as "appointed time." While these holy days are symbolic in nature, they do represent appointed times for events in the Kingdom of God.

The holy days of the Torah are divided into two sections. There is a group in the spring and a group in the autumn. These two groups are related to the two comings of the Messiah. The first coming of Yeshua is related to the spring holy days; the Second Coming is related to the autumn holy days.

It is not a coincidence that the three primary events of the first coming occurred during the spring holy days. Yeshua was crucified on Passover; He was raised from the dead on the first day of the Omer (first fruits); and the Holy Spirit was poured out on Shavuot (Pentecost). Those three holy days found their meaning and fulfillment in the events surrounding Yeshua's First Coming. In the same way, the three autumn holy days (Trumpets, Day of Atonement, and Tabernacles) will find their fulfillment in the events surrounding Yeshua's second coming.

Not only did Yeshua fulfill the spring holy days; He did it on the very day that the holy day was being celebrated. Even though the religious Jews might not have accepted Yeshua, the event still happened on the appointed time of the traditional biblical feast. The whole celebration of the Passover, for instance, was a prophetic action by the high priests, even if they didn't know it (see Jn. 11:51).

If the spring holy days were connected to the first coming, it stands to reason that the events of the Second Coming will be connected to the autumn holy days. If the events of the first coming occurred on the exact days of the traditional celebration of the spring holy days, it also stands to reason that the events of the Second Coming will occur on the exact days of the traditional celebration of the autumn holy days.

The Last Trumpet

The Feast of Trumpets finds its fulfillment in the seven trumpets of the Book of Revelation. They should not be confused with the "last trumpet." That is a different special trumpet, which is blown once every 50 years at the Jubilee.

Leviticus 25:9

You shall cause the trumpet of the Jubilee to sound on the tenth day of the seventh month; on the Day of Atonement you shall make the trumpet to sound throughout all your land.

In Jewish tradition, this trumpet is blown at sundown at the end of the Day of Atonement. (At this time it is blown every year as a remembrance.)

The seven trumpets of Revelation are a series of events leading up to the Second Coming. That is the fulfillment of the Feast of Trumpets. The "last trumpet" is sounded at the very moment of the second coming of Yeshua. It is the fulfillment of the Jubilee trumpet of the Day of Atonement. (That gives us a biblical hint that the second coming of Yeshua might take place at sundown on the Day of Atonement.)

This last trumpet is mentioned three times specifically in the New Testament.

Matthew 24:29-31

Immediately after the tribulation of those days...

They will see the Son of Man coming on the clouds of heaven...

He will send His angels with a great sound of a trumpet, and they will gather together His elect from the four winds, from one end of heaven to the other.

1 Corinthians 15:23,51-52
Each one in his own order: Christ the firstfruits, afterward those who are Christ's at His coming.

Behold I tell you a mystery: We shall not all sleep, but we shall all be changed—

in a moment, in the twinkling of an eye, at the last trumpet. For the trumpet will sound, and the dead will be raised incorruptible, and we shall be changed.

1 Thessalonians 4:15b-17a
We who are alive and remain until the coming of the Lord will by no means precede those who are asleep.

For the Lord Himself will descend from heaven with a shout... and with the trumpet of God. And the dead in Christ will rise first.

Then we who are alive and remain shall be caught up together with them in the clouds to meet the Lord in the air.

In all of these passages, the last trumpet heralds in three events:

1.   The second coming of Yeshua,

2.   The resurrection of the dead,

3.   The Rapture of the saints.

Those three events are connected one to another. They are all connected to the last trumpet. When Yeshua returns, the dead will be raised. There is no reason for them to be raised *before* He comes. When the dead are raised, then the believers who are alive at the time will have their bodies changed into the *same* resurrection type bodies.

Note: The Rapture is referring to a special event in which the believers in Yeshua will have their bodies changed into resurrection bodies and be swept up into the air to welcome Him at the Second Coming. Those new bodies will be eternal and will be appropriate for movement both on earth and in Heaven. (just as Yeshua Himself after the Resurrection was able to eat a meal with His disciples [see Jn. 21] and then be raised into the air [see Acts 1].)

There is no reason for the believers to have their bodies changed until the *same time* that the dead are raised. The dead are raised and the believers are changed for the *same reason*. Since it is for the same reason, it is at the same time. The power that Yeshua will use to conquer the world is the *same power* He will use to raise the dead and to transform the saints.

They all occur at the time of the sounding of the last trumpet. Therefore, they are also simultaneous one with another. The three events happen in a quick series, one immediately following the other, in this order: the Second Coming, the Resurrection, and the Rapture.

After The Tribulation

Unfortunately many dear Christians have believed a false doctrine that the Rapture occurs seven years before the Second Coming, i.e., before the Tribulation.

The preceding quotations from Matthew, First Corinthians, and Thessalonians are not obscure passages taken out of context. They are basic texts in the New Testament concerning the Second Coming. Much of the teaching on "pre-tribulation" Rapture uses references that are not primarily dealing with the subject.

It is important, when considering any principle of Scripture, to check what was Yeshua's foundational teaching on the subject. He clearly says, "After the tribulation of those days" (see Mt. 24:29). All the theologians in the world can tell me "before the Tribulation," but if Yeshua tells me, "after the Tribulation," I'd rather go with Him.

Let's look at the same teaching of Yeshua in Mark's gospel. Yeshua tells about wars, rumors of wars, and earthquakes. Then He says:

Mark 13:8b
There will be famines and troubles. These are the beginnings of sorrows.

We could call this the first stage of tribulation. The word *sorrows* here is like "birth pangs." The tribulation of the endtime is like birth pangs, which start slowly—with breaks in between—then get stronger and closer together.

John 16:21
A woman, when she is in labor, has sorrow because her hour has come; but as soon as she has given birth to the child, she no

longer remembers the anguish, for joy that a human being has been born into the world.

The end-time tribulation is like birth pangs, not only in the pace and intensity, but also in the goal: The pains are to give birth to something. They are bringing something positive into the world. The end-time tribulation gives birth to the second coming of Yeshua and the Kingdom of God on earth.

A woman might want to run away from her labor pains. But there can be no birth without the pain. The Tribulation is not something for believers to enjoy. However, it is not something for us to escape from either. The community of believers is the woman who will give the birth. We need to be here. It will be the most important task we will ever have.

Then Yeshua goes on to say that we will be betrayed by family members and hated by all nations. He describes this period as:

Mark 13:19
For in those days there will be tribulation such as has not been since the beginning of the creation...until this time, nor ever shall be.

This may be considered the fullness of the tribulation period. Yeshua does not say that we will be removed from that period. In fact, He says just the opposite; that we must endure through it to the end.

Mark 13:13b
He who endures to the end shall be saved.

All the verses from Mark 13:6 to Mark 13:23 are describing the Tribulation. Then Yeshua speaks of what will come "after" this tribulation.

Mark 13:24-27
In those days, after that tribulation, the sun will be darkened...

And the powers in the heavens will be shaken.

Then they will see the Son of Man coming in the clouds with great power...

Then He will send His angels, and gather together His elect from the four winds, from the farthest part of earth...

In verse 24, Yeshua says "after" that tribulation. In verse 26, He says "then" will be the Second Coming. In verse 27, He says "then" will be the gathering together of the elect. To quote the most pertinent part of the verses:

"after the tribulation… they will see the Son of Man coming… and gather together His elect." Here is the order again:

verse 8: beginning tribulation.

verse 19: great tribulation.

verse 24: after the Tribulation,

verse 26: the Second Coming,

verse 26: the Rapture.

Noah and Lot

Yeshua taught that the flood of Noah by water and the destruction of Sodom by fire are examples of the judgment that will occur at His second coming.

Luke 17:26,28

As it was in the days of Noah, so it will be also in the days of the Son of Man.

Likewise as it was also in the days of Lot…

The judgment at the Second Coming will be as large as Noah's flood. But instead of water the flood will be like the fire that destroyed Sodom (see 2Pet. 3). It will be like both of those judgments combined. What is scary is not just the degree of the destruction, but that so many people will be caught unaware. Just as it was in the days of Noah and Lot, most people will just scoff at the warnings of God. That is all the more reason for us to bring salvation to as many people as possible. The fear and love of God compel us (see 2 Cor. 5:11).

Noah and Lot were taken out of the way on the day that the total disaster came—not seven years before it. It was on the very day.

Luke 17:27,29

…until the day that Noah entered the ark…

On the day that Lot went out of Sodom…

The sequence is similar to what will happen at the Second Coming. The saints will be taken out of the way on the very day that the flood of fire falls. It is also similar to the Exodus. During the plagues, the children of Israel stayed in Egypt because God was warning the people. At the Red Sea, Pharaoh's armies were drowned in a moment. During the Tribulation, we need to be here as witnesses to unbelievers. When that time is finished, and the time for destruction is come, then we will be removed.

There is a difference between punishment and destruction. When God is ready to destroy the forces of evil, He can do it in a moment. It won't take seven years of tribulation. The tribulation punishments are a measure of His *grace* so that people will repent. During the punishment warnings, we will be here. At the destruction of the wicked, we will not. We stay as witnesses during the Tribulation; we are raptured as the "saved" at the Second Coming.

Parable of the Tares

Yeshua said that the Second Coming was like a man who planted wheat in his field, but an enemy planted tares. The two had to grow together until the harvest at the end. The wheat is the believers; the tares are the wicked.

Matthew 13:30b,40-43a
First gather together the tares and bind them in bundles to burn them, but gather the wheat into my barn.

Therefore as the tares are gathered and burned in the fire, so it will be at the end of this age.

The Son of Man will send out His angels, and they will gather out of His kingdom all things that offend, and those who practice lawlessness,

And will cast them into the furnace of fire. There will be wailing and gnashing of teeth.

Then the righteous will shine forth as the sun in the kingdom of their Father.

The righteous will shine forth like the sun when they get new resurrection bodies (at the Rapture). The wheat will be gathered into the barn at the Rapture. But these things will not happen until the same time that the wicked are destroyed—*not before*.

Don't Be Deceived

In His end-times teachings, Yeshua often warned about deception. Paul also warned specifically not to be deceived that the Rapture would come before the Tribulation:

2 Thessalonians 2:1,3
Now, brethren, concerning the coming of our Lord Jesus Christ and our gathering together to Him...

Let no one deceive you by any means; for that Day will not come unless the falling away comes first, and the man of sin is revealed, the son of perdition.

The subject of this passage is two items: the Second Coming and the Rapture. Those two key events will happen on the same day, "that Day." That Day will not happen until the great apostasy and the antichrist are revealed first. The apostasy and the antichrist are both tribulation events. If those events occur before the Second Coming and the Rapture, then obviously the Rapture happens after the Tribulation.

There are three levels of doctrinal error. The first is simply "error," which though incorrect, will not do much damage to the believers. The second level is "deception," which can do damage, but not cause them to lose their salvation. The third level is "blasphemy," which is serious enough to endanger a person's salvation.

Denying the resurrection of Yeshua, for instance, would be a blasphemy. Pre-tribulation rapture is not a blasphemy. However, it is a deception, since it can cause damage to a person's faith.

[Note: Michael Brown, Messianic Jewish scholar and director of FIRE school of ministry, points out that Second Thessalonians 1:7 states that the judgment of the wicked and the relief for the believers takes place during one and the same event—the second coming of Yeshua. If the relief of the believers takes place at the same time as the destruction of the wicked, there could be no rapture of the Church previous to that time.

In addition, all the Greek terms allegedly meant to describe the Rapture (*parousia*—which means 'visit, arrival"; *epiphania*—which means "shining forth"; and *apokalupsis*—which means "revealing") describe public visible events. They are not secret hidden events that don't actually arrive here.

Dr. Brown further notes that Isaiah 26:20 promises God's people to be hidden and protected during the time of His wrath, not to be removed. This prophecy is part of the larger context of Isaiah chapters 24–27, which describe the end-times tribulation, spiritual warfare, the Rapture, and the resurrection of the dead.]

Not Soldiers on Retreat

Yeshua is like an army commander trying to give instructions to His soldiers for a great battle. Some of the officers are giving contrary instructions that the soldiers should be preparing for a massive retreat. A soldier preparing for war is different from one who thinks he will be discharged shortly before the war begins (see 2 Tim. 2:3).

Many believers today are like soldiers who are looking forward to an early discharge. Can you imagine David or Joshua telling their soldiers to prepare to retreat at the last minute? Can you imagine Peter or Paul looking to escape from preaching because there was persecution on the way?

Acts 14:22
Strengthening the souls of the disciples, exhorting them to continue in the faith, and saying, "We must through many tribulations enter the Kingdom of God."

2 Timothy 3:12
All who desire to live godly in Christ Jesus will suffer persecution.

Yeshua prayed not that we should be taken out of the world, but that we should be protected by faith while in the world.

John 17:15
I do not pray that You should take them out of the world, but that You should keep them from the evil one.

Yeshua calls us to be faithful unto death (see Phil. 2:8; Rev. 2:10; 12:10). If we are to be faithful unto death, how much more should we be faithful through tribulation? The Bible portrays believers who will praise God even during the last judgments of the bowls of wrath (see Rev. 15:2). If it is possible to have victory even despite the persecution of the beast, why should the body of believers have to be removed before that time?

The Bible speaks of the two great witnesses, who will be lifted up into Heaven (see Rev. 11:12). The whole world is surprised by this event. This happens at the sounding of the seventh trumpet. It is obvious that a billion Christians could not have been raptured previous to this time. The rapture of the two witnesses is a sign to the world to repent, and a sign to the believers to get ready. So the Rapture must happen *after* the time of the two witnesses.

Perseverance and Faith

Perhaps the worst picture of tribulation in the whole Bible is found in Revelation 13. There the beast and the antichrist seem to have taken control over the whole world. At that worst of times, God calls His people to persevere.

Revelation 13:10b
Here is the [perseverance] *and the faith of the saints.*

At that time we are to "hang in there," to persevere, to have faith. There is no talk of escaping. If here at the peak of the beast tribulation, the believers are to be there, how could anyone say we would be raptured before that? The only potential answer is that those believers are different: "Those are tribulation believers and we are pre-tribulation believers."

What self-deception! If they are different saints, what is different about them? Do they have a different Yeshua, a different Holy Spirit, a different faith? Of course not. If it is not for believers to go through tribulation, why wouldn't all the new believers during the Tribulation be raptured immediately? No. We are the faithful and we are called to persevere over persecution.

1 Thessalonians 4:15b
We who are alive and remain until the coming of the Lord will by
no means precede those who are asleep.

It was the same "we" even back in the time of Paul. There are not two different groups of saints. "We" do not precede by seven years the resurrection of the dead. "We" will be here until the coming of Yeshua. We "remain." At that time the dead in Messiah will be raised, and we will be raptured.

Until then our goal is evangelism, not evacuation. Our eyes are on the triumph, not the tribulation.

CHAPTER 14

SPIRITUAL WARFARE IN THE ENDTIMES

God wants to protect us during tribulation. We will receive a seal of protection from the Holy Spirit so that the disasters of the endtimes cannot touch us. Here is the instruction of the angels:

Revelation 7:3
Do not harm the earth, the sea, or the trees till we have sealed the servants of our God on their foreheads.

When the plagues of God came upon Egypt, there was a supernatural protection on the people in Goshen. The flies could not touch them (see Ex. 8:22). Their livestock were not hurt by the pestilence (see Ex. 9:4,6). The hail did not fall on them (see Ex. 9:26). When thick darkness fell on all the land, there was supernatural light inside the houses of the children of Israel (see Ex. 10:23). And the blood of the lamb protected their children from harm (see Ex. 12:13).

How much more can the blood of the Lamb protect us today!

Revelation 12:11
They overcame [the accuser] *by the blood of the Lamb and by the word of their testimony, and they did not love their lives to the death.*

That's the attitude we need for the endtimes. It is possible to overcome even the worst attacks of the devil. We have divine protection by the blood of the Lamb. And we will persevere through every trial, being faithful even unto death.

This protection was not just a defensive measure. The plagues were seen as God's judgment upon Egypt and its gods (see Ex. 12:12). It was an offensive tactic of God to show His glory and dominion (see Ex. 6:6). So will it be that the judgments of the endtimes will demonstrate God's power and justice. They are miraculous signs and wonders.

These miraculous signs and wonders are part of the outpouring of God's Spirit in the end-times right before the second coming of Yeshua.

Acts 2:17,19-20 (See also Joel 2:28-31)
It shall come to pass in the last days, says God, that I will pour out of My Spirit on all flesh...

I will show wonders in heaven above and signs in the earth beneath; blood and fire and vapor of smoke.

The sun shall be turned into darkness, and the moon into blood, before the coming of the great and awesome day of the Lord.

Not only are these judgments part of the revival, but also they will cause many people to be saved.

Acts 2:21 (See also Joel 2:32a)
And it shall come to pass that whoever calls on the name of the Lord shall be saved.

The miraculous signs and wonders of the endtimes, both the healings and the judgments, will cause people to turn to the Lord. It's all part of the last outpouring of the Holy Spirit. It will be our job to help people come to the Lord during that time.

The Devil's Panic

We are not the chased; we are the chasers. The reason that the Tribulation at that time will be so intense is that the devil knows he is *losing*.

Revelation 12:12b
Woe to the inhabitants of the earth and the sea! For the devil has come down to you, having great wrath, because he knows that he has a short time.

Yes, the devil has great wrath. Yes, it will be difficult for us. But why is the devil wrathful? Because he knows his time is running out. How come the devil knows he is losing, and most of us don't know that? He is a cornered snake. This is the end of the game. The devil loses, and he is a "sore loser." The reason for the Tribulation is that the devil is panicking. He has been thrown down. Let's throw him down; all the way down into the abyss (see Rev. 20).

The Tribulation is the culmination of the spiritual warfare that has been going on since the fall of Adam. Because of the sin of humans and the rebellion of demons, there has always been opposition to the will of God.

That makes for conflict. Whenever the Kingdom of God advances, there is an equal and opposite reaction by the forces of evil. The darkness hates the light.

Moses brought the judgments into Egypt. Paul and his team caused earthquakes (Acts 16) and riots (Acts 19), and literally turned the world upside down (Acts 17:6). God gathers our prayers like incense and throws them down to the earth in fiery judgments.

Revelation 8:3-5

Another angel, having a golden censer, came and stood at the altar. He was given much incense, that he should offer it with the prayers of all the saints upon the golden altar which was before the throne.

And the smoke of the incense, with the prayers of the saints, ascended before God from the angel's hand.

Then the angel took the censer, filled it with fire from the altar, and threw it to the earth. And there were noises, thunderings, lightnings, and an earthquake.

We are not passive spectators of the endtimes; we are active players. We are the victors, not the victims. Our prayers rise before God like incense. In Heaven they are changed into power and thrown by angels back onto the earth. That causes the end-times signs and wonders.

Even though the nations of the world will attack Jerusalem out of evil intention (see Ezek. 38:12), it is God Himself who says, "I will gather all the nations to battle against Jerusalem" (Zech. 14:2a). The Bible says that God "sits in the heavens and laughs" (see Ps. 2:4), when He looks at the rebellion of the nations. It's as if He is saying, "Make My day!" God is not trying to avoid a conflict. It's only because of His mercy that He holds back His power (see 2 Pet. 3:9).

Prayers Affect History

We dare to believe that our prayers can affect history. Daniel is a great example: He searched the Scriptures and learned that Jeremiah had prophesied that the time for the restoration of Israel was at hand.

Daniel 9:2-3a

...I, Daniel, understood by the books the number of the years specified by the word of the Lord through Jeremiah the prophet,

that He would accomplish seventy years in the desolations of Jerusalem.

Then I set my face toward the Lord God to make request by prayer and supplications.

The first step in spiritual warfare is to study the Scriptures. We have to pray according to the guidelines in the Word of God. We take what is written in the Bible, and through prayer, help to bring it to pass in our generation.

We believe that angels affect history, and that our prayers affect angels. After Daniel prayed for 21 days, an angelic figure appeared to him.

Daniel 10:12
Do not fear, Daniel, for from the first day that you set your heart to understand, and to humble yourself before your God, your words were heard; and I have come because of your words.

From the moment we start praying, angels move into action. Even one person who humbles himself can change history. Human words of prayer, particularly combined with fasting, can mobilize angelic forces. It may take a while to see results, but the action starts immediately.

Daniel 10:13a
The prince of the kingdom of Persia withstood me twenty-one days; and behold, Michael, one of the chief princes, came to help me.

There was an invisible battle raging exactly the same number of days that Daniel prayed. The moment we start praying, the angels start fighting for us. The moment we stop praying, they stop fighting.

Daniel 10:20b
I must return to fight with the prince of Persia, and when I have gone forth, indeed the prince of Greece will come.

During the time of Jeremiah, Babylon ruled the world. During Daniel's time the world power changed from Babylon to Persia. In the generation following Daniel, Greece rose in power to conquer the Middle East. Just as those changes in history were affected by the prayers of Jeremiah and Daniel, so can our prayers be effective today.

Spiritual Warfare

How does this happen? In the beginning God gave delegated authority over the earth to mankind (see Gen. 1:28; Ps. 8:6; 115:16). He also gave us free will. Our prayers have an effect on this planet because of that spiritual authority. Unfortunately, all of us have sinned. Many of the angels have sinned as well. Approximately one-third of the angels joined satan in rebellion against God. Now the evil angels and the good angels fight against one another.

Revelation 12:4,7-9

[The dragon's] *tail drew a third of the stars of heaven and threw them to the earth.*

And war broke out in heaven: Michael and his angels fought with the dragon; and the dragon and his angels fought,

But they did not prevail, nor was a place found for them in heaven any longer.

So the great dragon was cast out, that serpent of old, called the devil and Satan, who deceives the whole world; he was cast to the earth, and his angels were cast out with him.

The angels who sinned were punished by God, being bound in chains of darkness.

They were restricted and confined to areas of spiritual darkness. Demonic powers have no right to gain access or dominion on the earth.

2 Peter 2:4

...God did not spare the angels who sinned, but cast them down to hell and delivered them into chains of darkness, to be reserved for judgment.

However, when human beings sin, they give access to the demonic powers. Sin causes spiritual darkness. Spiritual darkness is a state of mental blindness. When that blindness reigns in the minds of men, demons have full influence on their minds. Through that darkness, demons can gain dominion over human society.

If people turn back to God, they receive new light of truth and understanding. The strongholds of demonic spirits are broken down.

2 Corinthians 10:4-5
The weapons of our warfare are not carnal but mighty in God for
pulling down strongholds,

Casting down arguments and every high thing that exalts itself
against the knowledge of God, bringing every thought captive to
the obedience of Christ.

When a person repents, light comes into his mind and the demonic
strongholds are pulled down. When we preach and confront wrong thinking, we can change the minds of men, and thereby tear down the evil strongholds. Tearing down evil structures in the thoughts of men tears down the
base of demonic influence. When the light of revelatory truth comes into
our minds, we know that a spiritual victory has been won and that demonic
strongholds have been pulled down. The spiritual victory, the revelation in
our thoughts, and the breakthrough of angelic forces all go together.

Dividing Satan's Kingdom

Spiritual warfare then is done on two levels—prayer and preaching.
Yeshua gave us authority over all evil spiritual forces.

Luke 10:19a
I give you the authority to trample on serpents and scorpions,
and over all the power of the enemy.

When we pray in faith, we can use spiritual authority to bind demonic forces and mobilize angelic forces. Our prayers influence the warfare between the angels and demons. The activity of angels and demons affects
human society and history. Therefore, our prayers have an influence on society and history as well.

One of the first rules of spiritual warfare, taught by Yeshua, is dividing the forces of the enemy. It is a very high priority to maintain unity in a
local congregation. Divisions among believers go hand in hand with the attacks of the devil. Laying down your life to maintain unity in the congregation is part of fighting spiritual warfare.

Luke 11:17b-18
Every kingdom divided against itself is brought to desolation,
and a house divided against a house falls.

If Satan also is divided against himself, how will his kingdom
stand?

One day, as I was meditating on this passage, I realized that it also could be used as a weapon against the devil. If satan's kingdom is divided, it will not be able to stand. We have authority to bind demons. Why could we not use that authority to pray division into satan's kingdom?

I decided to try it. I began to pray by faith and declare, "Satan's kingdom is divided and fallen." As I said that, I had a vision in my heart. The ground beneath me turned to glass, and I could see down into the kingdom of satan. My words were being broadcast on a loud speaker throughout the corridors of hell. Satan and all of his forces were paralyzed and forced to listen.

Although demonic ranks have a hierarchy under satan, their unity is only held together by fear and hatred. There is no essential unity or loyalty among them. They would be more than willing to destroy one another. Our prayers to bring division into the ranks of satan's forces can have tremendous power and effectiveness.

Casting out a demon brings deliverance to one person. Praying for division among satan's forces can cause them to fight among themselves. It can bring destruction and confusion on multitudes of demons. The effect is exponential.

A survey of Scripture shows how important this strategy is in winning spiritual battles. The forces of the Philistines were divided among themselves when Jonathan attacked them (see 1 Sam. 14:20). When Jehoshaphat's people sang praises to the Lord, the armies of Moab and Edom fought against one another (see 2 Chron. 20:23). When Gideon attacked the camp of the Midianites, the enemy soldiers began to attack one another (see Judg. 7:22). When Paul was attacked by the religious leaders, he called for a division among the Sadducees and the Pharisees (see Acts 23:6-7). In the endtimes, the beast will turn against the harlot of Babylon and destroy it (see Rev. 17:16).

This was the method that Ezekiel tells us to use in prophesying against the forces of Gog and Magog:

Ezekiel 38:21

"I will call for a sword against Gog throughout all My mountains," says the Lord God. "Every man's sword will be against his brother."

I urge you to make this prayer of dividing satan's kingdom a regular part of your spiritual warfare strategy. Let us claim by faith, "Satan's kingdom is divided and fallen."

Gathered to Jerusalem

Let us look again at the three New Testament passages that speak of the "last great trumpet."

Matthew 24:30b-31

They will see the Son of Man coming on the clouds of heaven...

And He will send His angels with a great sound of a trumpet, and they will gather together His elect from the four winds, from one end of heaven to the other.

1 Corinthians 15:23b,51-52

Christ the firstfruits, afterward those who are Christ's at His coming.

Behold, I tell you a mystery: We shall not all sleep, but we shall all be changed—

in a moment, in the twinkling of an eye, at the last trumpet. For the trumpet will sound, and the dead will be raised incorruptible, and we shall be changed.

1 Thessalonians 4:16-17a

The Lord Himself will descend from heaven with a shout... and with the trumpet of God. And the dead in Christ will rise first.

Then we who are alive and remain shall be caught up together with them in the clouds to meet the Lord in the air.

As we mentioned earlier, all of these passages speak of the second coming of Yeshua, of the Rapture of the believers, and of the resurrection of the dead. Those three great events are tied together symbolically by the "last great trumpet" to the Day of Atonement from Leviticus 25:9, and to the "great and [terrible] day of the Lord" in Joel 2:31.

The "last great trumpet" of the New Testament is primarily a quote from Isaiah. The passage in Isaiah does not speak of being swept into the air, although its context does speak of the resurrection (see Is. 26:19) and of the destruction of satan (see Is. 27:1). Rather it speaks of being gathered to Jerusalem.

Isaiah 27:13

So it shall be in that day; the great trumpet will be blown; they will come, who are about to perish in the land of Assyria, and they who are outcasts in the land of Egypt, and shall worship the Lord in the holy mount of Jerusalem.

The gathering of the people to Jerusalem fits perfectly with the vision of Isaiah 2 of world peace, with its center in Zion; with the vision of the dry bones in Ezekiel 37, in which the resurrected will be brought to Israel; with the vision in Ezekiel 40, in which the survivors of the battle of Gog will rebuild the temple; and with the vision in Zechariah 14, in which the nations that survive will come to worship in Jerusalem.

The New Testament passage does not mention where the believers will be gathered to once they have been swept into the air. It only says, they will "meet" the Lord in the air. Given the context of the Hebrew prophets, it might be assumed that the raptured saints would be taken to Jerusalem.

Many do not see it that way. They understand that in the Rapture, they will be taken up all the way into Heaven. In some ways that is not logical, by the mere fact that Yeshua is on His way down to set up His kingdom on earth. It's as if they are going to pass Him by on an escalator: As they go up, He comes down.

1 Thessalonians 4:17

We who are alive and remain shall be caught up together with them in the clouds to meet the Lord in the air. And thus we shall always be with the Lord.

This passage does not say where we will stay. It only says that we will meet the Lord in the air, and always be with Him. Now there are two options: One is to go back with Yeshua to dwell in Heaven. The other is to welcome Him into earthly Jerusalem and dwell with Him here.

The word for meet in verse 17 is the Greek word *apentesis*. It is used in Matthew 25 in the parable of the ten virgins, who go out to meet and welcome in the bridegroom. It is also used in Acts 28:15, when the believers go out of the city to the Appii forum in order to welcome Paul into Rome. In both of those passages, the meaning is not for those going out to leave with the guest, but to welcome him in and return with him to their home.

So which one is it?

Two Resurrections

To solve this problem, we must realize that the New Testament speaks of two resurrections, one at the beginning of the millennial reign and the other at the end.

Revelation 20:4b-5

I saw the souls of those who had been beheaded for their witness to Jesus and for the word of God, who had not worshiped the beast or his image, and had not received his mark on their fore-heads or on their hands. And they lived and reigned with Christ for a thousand years.

But the rest of the dead did not live again until the thousand years were finished. This is the first resurrection.

At the first resurrection, those who had lost their lives for Yeshua will live and reign with Him in this earth for a thousand years. They will be leaders in His kingdom and help to prepare the world for the final stage of paradise. The rest of the people will be part of the second resurrection. At that resurrection, the wicked will be punished in the lake of fire (see Rev. 20:15). The righteous will descend out of Heaven to be part of the eternal paradise, when Heaven and earth are joined in harmony (see Rev. 21:1-4).

The first resurrection is for a select group of the righteous only. The second resurrection is for the rest of the righteous and for the wicked. Those of the righteous in the second resurrection will be waiting in Heaven during the millennial reign of Yeshua, and then descend with heavenly Jerusalem at the end of the Millennium.

It is not my purpose here to analyze which of the righteous will be in the first or second resurrections. Certainly not all of them will be in the first resurrection, since most will descend to earth as part of the "Bride" at the end of the Millennium. In addition, the blessed privilege of the martyrs to be part of the first resurrection (see Rev. 20) would not make sense, if all of the righteous would be there anyway.

In the Millennium, some of the believers will be on the earth, and some in Heaven.

Martyrdom

It should be our goal to make it to the first resurrection. That is the more blessed option. If that means being physically martyred for Yeshua, so be it. If it means having a total dedication as if spiritually martyred, so be it. In any case we need to purpose in our hearts to be faithful unto death (see Acts 7:55-60; Phil. 2:7-9; 3:10; Rev. 2:10; 11:7; 7:14; 20:4; Heb. 11:35-37; John 21:19). This is the highest level of ministry success a believer can attain.

It was the hope of Paul, that he might be martyred to attain the first resurrection.

Philippians 3:10b-11
Being conformed to His death,

If by any means, I may attain to the resurrection from the dead.

Paul was not doubting his salvation here, nor was he saying that any-one who isn't martyred cannot be saved. What he desired was to attain a higher level at the resurrection through martyrdom and to be part of the first resurrection. The same principle is applied to many heroes of faith:

Hebrews 11:35b
Others were tortured, not accepting deliverance, that they might obtain a better resurrection.

What a different attitude they had than most of us do! May God grant us that kind of total faith and dedication, even unto martyrdom! That is the ultimate victory in spiritual warfare.

CHAPTER 15

O COLUMBIA, O PALESTINE

Sometimes we charismatics can get a little "spooky" by looking at every event as a sign from Heaven. It borders on being superstitious. On the other hand, it's difficult not to see the biblical symbolism in the events connected with the Columbia space shuttle disaster. There was too much to overlook or chalk off as mere coincidence.

Here were some of the elements:

- *Columbia*—The name *Columbia* represents the American dream of "life, liberty, and the pursuit of happiness." (Columbia, of course, taken from the name Columbus, who "discovered the new world.")

- *Palestine*—The first reports of the shuttle's disintegration were from "over" Palestine, Texas.

- *Heavenlies*—The space program was in the "heavenlies," which biblically represents spiritual authority and dominion.

- *Texas*—Is obviously the home of George W. Bush, and the home of some major American oil interests as well.

- *Falling star*—The shuttle appeared to be a star falling out of heaven when it disintegrated. A falling star is also the sign of the fall of a world power.

- *Seven flags*—The crew was made up of six Americans and one Israeli, symbolizing the partnership between America and Israel.

- *Iraq-Ramon Connection*—In 1981 Israel bombed the Iraqi nuclear reactor outside of Baghdad. The reactor was part of Saddam Hussein's effort to build nuclear weapons. Israel felt it had no choice but to make that preemptive strike. It was an incredible risk, but turned out to be phenomenally successful. (Looking back over the years, one shudders to think what would have happened in the '91 Gulf War had Hussein had nuclear weapons in his possession.) Israel sent a small squadron of F-16 fighter planes. How did eight Israeli planes fly right up to Baghdad? They flew in such a tight pattern that they appeared, on Iraqi radar, to be one large passenger plane. One of the pilots leading the mission was the young Ilan Ramon, who later became the Israeli astronaut on the Columbia shuttle.

The successful bombing by Ilan Ramon of the Iraqi reactor took place ten years before the Gulf War with President Bush senior. The Columbia space shuttle disaster took place right before the war on Iraq with President Bush junior.

The Big "IF"

Sometimes a small symbolic defeat can be a warning of a potentially larger defeat close at hand.

Esther 6:13b

If Mordecai, before whom you have begun to fall, is of Jewish descent, you will not prevail against him but will surely fall before him.

In this passage Haman's wife, Zeresh, warns him that his humbling experience before Mordecai is a spiritual sign that he is about to have a bigger fall. In the Columbia shuttle disaster, the symbolism was somewhat reversed.

Although not prophecy, the symbolism of the event had a seemingly quite sober meaning, at least on the surface. The Columbia crashed. The message was twofold:

- That the United States (and Israel with it) stands to suffer a humiliating defeat in attacking Iraq.

- That the United States and Israeli partnership stands to disintegrate over the Palestinian issue.

This was not a judgment, but a warning. In other words, the defeat was not decreed to happen. The shuttle disaster was a symbolic warning of what could happen if there is not appropriate prayer and repentance. The scales could be tipped in either direction.

God is calling the believers in Israel, America, and around the world to give themselves much more to intercessory prayer and moral repentance in the light of the huge and impending conflicts of the endtimes. I believe God wants to give victory to America, to Israel, and to countries wherever the gospel is strong. He wants to remove dictatorships and destroy regimes that support terror. He wants to strengthen righteousness in nations and weaken unrighteousness. However, those things are not going to happen without spiritual warfare.

There is a big "IF."

2 Chronicles 7:14

If My people who are called by My name will humble themselves, and pray and seek My face, and turn from their wicked ways, then I will hear from heaven, and will forgive their sin and heal their land.

The solution is clearly humility, godliness, and repentance. Spiritual warfare is not just claiming our authority to bind and loose. Spiritual battle starts first on the pride and lusts of our own hearts.

When we submit ourselves to God, the devil has to submit to us (see Jas. 4:7). As we humble ourselves before God, the devil will have to flee from us (see 1 Pet. 5:6,9). The word of the Lord is a *two*-edged sword (see Heb. 4:12). First we have to use it on ourselves. Sometimes it is easier for us to "stab" someone else than it is to "cut" the carnality out of our own lives.

So what do we need to repent of?

Jehoshaphat

Some of the prophetic ministries coming from Christian Zionists and Messianic Jews place an emphasis on criticizing leftist or moderate political leaders in America and Israel for their stated willingness to allow for a Palestinian state. They point out that a Palestinian state would be tantamount to the sin of "dividing up God's holy land."

Joel 3:1-2

For behold, in those days and at that time, when I bring back the captives of Judah and Jerusalem,

I will also gather all nations, and bring them down to the Valley of Jehoshaphat; and I will enter into judgment with them there

on account of My people, My heritage Israel, whom they have
scattered among the nations; they have also divided up My land.

The failure of the nations to recognize God's covenant with Israel—
that the land of Israel belongs to the Jewish people, is a great sin. It is such
a great sin that it is part of what leads up to the very battle of Armageddon
at the second coming of Yeshua. We believe strongly in defending Israel's
right to live in this land, including militarily. (That's why we see our children's service in the Israeli army as part of their service to the Lord.)

The passage in Joel mentions two specific sins that bring the total
judgment of God upon the nations. One is their mistreatment of the Jews
during the two-thousand-year exile from the land. The exile was punishment
from God. The mistreatment of the Jews was sin on the part of the Gentiles
(see Zech. 1:15). That's what we call anti-Semitism. The battle of Armageddon (or Jehoshaphat) is seen as God's punishment on the nations.
Anti-Semitism is one of the major reasons for that punishment.

[The name *Jehoshaphat* means "Jehovah judges," just as the name
Jesus (*Jehoshua*) means "Jehovah saves." The Messiah's name in the first
coming was *Jehoshua*—He came to save. At the second, He will be coming
to judge as indicated by the name *Jehoshaphat* (see Rev. 19:12). The battle
of Armageddon in the valley of Jehoshaphat is where Yeshua will judge and
punish the nations.]

Joel also specifically mentions the "dividing" of the land. Almost all
of the political solutions for peace in the Middle East have involved "parti-
tion," which is, in effect, dividing the land. Again, that division may be
looked at from two angles. From Israel's side, the dividing of the land is
punishment for unrighteousness. From the side of the nations, taking away
the land from the Jewish people, to whom God promised it, is sinful. God
may have removed the Jews from the land for breaking the covenant, but
that does not mean that He covenanted to give it to someone else.

Taking the Speck Out

God's covenant with our people about the land of Israel is absolute.
However, the issue here has a lot more to it than simply right-wing politics
or Zionist ideology. We need to ask ourselves, "What is God saying to us as
believers in Yeshua?" Ownership of the land is one of the important issues.
However, viewing the occupation of the land as the *only* issue gives an un-
balanced perspective. The situation is much more complex than that.

Another problem of the "land only" view is that it does not involve humility and repentance on our part.

We read above in Second Chronicles 7:14 that the solution lies within us, as the people of God, the "people who are called by My name." We cannot just point the finger at the politicians and the Muslims. We have to deal with our own sin. If we will deal with our own sin, then God will hear from Heaven and heal the rest of the land. We deal with spiritual sins within the community of faith, and God takes care of the issues concerning the land and the politics.

Matthew 7:3

Why do you look at the speck in your brother's eye, but do not consider the plank in your own eye?

Our job is to humble ourselves, to pray, to seek God's face, and to repent. Humbling ourselves means to remove pride. We need to remove spiritual pride, intellectual pride, religious pride, theological pride, nationalist pride, and ethnic pride. We as Americans and Israelis don't realize how big this plank is in our eyes, and how easily it is seen by others. (I say that as one who has dual citizenship, both American and Israeli—and quite proud of it!)

We are to pray. In this case, prayer means prayer together with fasting. The times are urgent, and we need to give ourselves to prayer and fasting. The prayer and fasting of the people of Nineveh saved the city from impending disaster and judgment (see Jon. 3:5-10).

We are to seek His face. We have heard the expression that we need "to seek God's face instead of His hand." If we seek the victory, the victory will elude us. If we seek God's face instead of the victory, He will give us the victory anyway.

There is a subtle deception in the Western Christian world (including us Messianic Jews), in which we have taught the Bible as a system of spiritual principles through which we can be blessed. I believe in God's total blessing, prosperity, and victory. However, we have put more emphasis on the principles than on the "principal." We have missed the central focus of our personal relationship with God through Yeshua and His work on the cross. It has rightly been said, "You can't get the crown without taking up the cross."

We are called to turn from our wicked ways. Most of the world does not look at Israel and America as holding higher standards of integrity. What they see is lust and greed. We broadcast sexual immorality all over the world through media and entertainment, yet we expect the world to see us as holy. We are riddled with scandals and corruption in politics and business, yet we expect the world to see us as righteous.

Matthew 6:33
Seek first the Kingdom of God and His righteousness, and all these things shall be added unto you.

Our job is to seek God and His higher standards of moral purity. Then He will take care of the blessings.

Our first job is to preach the gospel. Our "occupying of the land" today is not done primarily by physical settlement, but by preaching the Kingdom of God. Some Messianic Jewish and Christian Zionist ministries have lowered their emphasis on evangelism, and therefore have overemphasized the issues of the land.

Yeshua said He would restore Israel as we concentrated on the baptism of the Holy Spirit and witnessing for the gospel (see Acts 1:8). I am one hundred percent for the prophecies of the restoration of Zion, but we have to keep evangelism as a higher priority. My children carry guns to defend against terrorists, but more importantly, they carry the witness of Yeshua and the gospel of eternal salvation.

Get the Sin Out

Two examples of hindrance to military victory stand out in the Bible. The first is the sin of Achan at Ai. God told Joshua that they had suffered defeat because there was sin in the camp. If they would remove that sin, victory would come.

Joshua 7:11
Israel has sinned, and they have also transgressed My covenant which I commanded them. For they have even taken some of the accursed things, and have both stolen and deceived; and they have also put it among their own stuff.

We have not only the sins of pride and lust as mentioned above, but also of greed. This passage is taking place within the "camp" of the covenant believers. I am not pointing a finger here at the outside world, but at us, as Messianic Jews and evangelical Christians, particularly those of us in "full-time" ministry. We have lacked integrity in dealing with the tithes and offerings of the Lord's people. We have used it for our own pleasure instead of evangelism, discipleship, and helping the poor. Many have raised money with slogans and pictures about Israel, but very little of it ends up in the hands of the local believers.

David established a rule that there would be equal portions for those who go to the battle and for those who sit by the stuff (see 1 Sam. 30:24-25 KJV). How much more should those who deal with fundraising share equally with those on the field! Ministries that receive donations connected with the issue of Israel need to share equal portions of those funds with local believers who maintain their faith in the difficult conditions here, yet have no avenues of fundraising.

Gibeonites and Palestinians

The second story of hindrance to victory is the Gibeonites. God told David that He would not bless him unless he made amends with the Gibeonites. The Gibeonites were natural enemies of Israel, but they had made a treaty with Israel through Joshua. Saul, in his mistaken and carnal zeal, attacked and killed the Gibeonites.

2 Samuel 21:1b-3

And the Lord answered, "It is because of Saul and his bloodthirsty house, because he killed the Gibeonites."

So the king called the Gibeonites and spoke to them. Now the Gibeonites were not of the children of Israel, but of the remnant of the Amorites; the children of Israel had sworn protection to them, but Saul had sought to kill them in his zeal for the children of Israel and Judah.

Therefore David said to the Gibeonites, "What shall I do for you? And with what shall I make atonement, that you may bless the inheritance of the Lord?"

David's job was to conquer the land. David represents the community of faith in the remnant of Israel. Saul represents the carnal version of David's kingdom. I see Saul as the unsaved Israeli community, particularly the over-zealous, right wing, ultra-orthodox. David had to make atonement for what Saul had done, even though it was not David's fault. In this passage about the Gibeonites, I see a parallel to the Palestinian Christians. While ethnically we are different, and politically we often find ourselves in fierce opposition, we have a covenant with them through Yeshua, just as the Gibeonites had a covenant with David through Joshua.

I remember watching Yaakov Damkani, a great sabra Israeli evangelist, weeping in prayer for God's mercy on the Palestinians, and particularly for the Palestinian Christians. Our hearts must be broken in love and compassion for the Palestinian people.

Jack Sara is a young, anointed Palestinian pastor and evangelist. I once asked him, "What do you want us as Israeli Messianic Jews to know?" Here are some of the burdens of his heart:

> "We are on fire for our people to be saved. We try to avoid the political issues. We want to know that that is your desire as well. Sometimes we think that the land is more important to you than the eternal salvation of our people.

> "We have a challenge when we share the gospel. Many Muslims get the impression from evangelists they see on cable television that evangelical Christianity is a political movement that supports Zionism and is anti-Arab. When we tell them we believe in Jesus, they think we are traitors or collaborators. They have trouble seeing the spiritual message because of the politics.

> "I can understand the security needs of the Israeli people to defend the civilians from harm. On the other hand, many of the measures end up humiliating and abusing the entire population of Palestinians. All of us know what it means to be humiliated and abused at the hands of Israeli soldiers.

> "I can also understand how important to you is what you believe about the prophecies concerning the endtime and God's dealing with Israel. Yet it seems to us that you often interpret those prophecies in a specific political agenda. You apply those prophecies to immediate political situations, which are out of balance with the wider spiritual issues of the Kingdom of God.

> "Sometimes we get the feeling that the greater Christian world does not know that we as Palestinian Christians even exist. People speak of Palestinians as if we were all terrorists. Do Christian Zionists have more of a sense of covenant with unsaved, right wing, Israeli settlers than they do with us, as born-again brothers and sisters in Jesus?

"We live in the midst of our people. What happens to them, happens to us. Our economy is collapsing, the people are suffering, and the closures have restricted us from normal living activities. Our evangelistic outreaches are based at this point on bringing basic food items to hundreds and hundreds of families."

I believe that we Messianic Jews have a mandate to stand with the Palestinian Christians both in prayer and in finances.

Land for Peace?

On the one hand, the Bible contains lengthy descriptions of the military conquest of the land of Israel. On the other hand, the forefathers often chose peaceful relationships with their neighbors by willingness to make concessions on land issues. Abraham gave the better part of the land to Lot in order not to argue (see Gen. 13). Isaac constantly moved out of the way when there were disputes over water rights in Israel (see Gen. 26). Jacob finally made peace with Esau by conceding almost all of his rights to land occupation (see Gen. 33).

The most influential rabbi in Israel for almost two decades has been Ovadia Yosef, leader of the ultra-orthodox Shas party. He made a rabbinic ruling that "pikuach nephesh," saving of human lives, is more important in the Torah than issues of the land. For this reason, although most of the orthodox are very right wing, they were willing to go along with peace treaty discussions.

Are human rights more important than occupying the land? Yes. Would we trade land for peace? Yes. Of course the question is not that simple. Making land concessions often seems to encourage terrorism and lead to the possibility of greater war. Land concessions for peace is biblical. Land concessions for a false peace treaty that leads to greater bloodshed is not biblical.

Without the basis for interracial reconciliation and forgiveness that is expressed by the crucifixion of Yeshua, there is no possibility for lasting peace in the Middle East. The Jewish society in Israel and the Muslim society of the Palestinians do not have the conceptual framework for making peace with one another. There is just vengeance. There is no solution without the gospel.

Jacob, Esau, and Peniel

Part of the problem is also demographic. The Jewish and Arab populations are interwoven in their villages and settlements. At the time of this writing there are more than three million Arabs and five and one-half million Jews living in Israel and the territories. There is no way to put up a fence that will neatly divide the two peoples. We are like two twin babies having a wrestling match in the womb of the same mother.

Genesis 25:21b-23

Rebecca [Isaac's] *wife conceived.*

But the children struggled together within her; and she said, "If all is well, why am I like this?" So she went to inquire of the Lord.

And the Lord said to her: "Two nations are in your womb, two peoples shall be separated from your body..."

After all these thousands of years, it seems that Jacob and Esau are still wrestling in the same womb.

In the Bible, Jacob represents the people of Israel. For 20 years Jacob was expelled from the land. That expulsion may be seen as symbolic of the two-thousand-year exile of the Jews from Israel. When Jacob returned to Israel, he had a life changing spiritual experience. He wrestled all night with a divine Man. He said of that Man, "I have seen the face of God" (see Gen. 32:30).

I believe that Man was the pre-incarnate Messiah, and Jacob's experience was symbolic of being born-again. This also refers to a wider experience, that as the exile of the Jewish people has come to an end in our generation, so are hundreds of thousands of Jewish people beginning to wrestle with the person of Yeshua and coming to a "born-again" faith in Him.

In the episode of Jacob's wrestling with the divine Man at Peniel, the context is Jacob's impending meeting with his brother Esau. The possibility of Esau's killing him made Jacob search for the Lord. The stress of the situation ironically led to his salvation experience. Then Jacob and Esau were reconciled. It was Jacob's wrestling with the Man of Peniel that led to the reconciliation with Esau.

So it is today, both for Israelis and Palestinians, that the Man of Galilee is the one who can bring us to reconciliation. In fact, Jacob said that it was through this difficult reconciliation with Esau that he received a greater revelation about the nature of God.

Genesis 33:10

...I have seen your face as though I had seen the face of God, and you were pleased with me.

It is possible for Jews and Arabs to be reconciled with one another. It is possible for them to love one another and even be "pleased" with one another through the gospel.

Genesis 33:4

Esau ran to meet him, and embraced him, and fell on his neck and kissed him, and they wept.

Reconciliation between Israelis and Palestinians is a necessary element of the message of the gospel, the witness of the gospel and the result of the gospel.

A Final Note

Investigation indicated that a small piece had broken off the Columbia space shuttle at takeoff. That little piece, though almost unnoticed, may have caused the damaged that ultimately destroyed the shuttle. The astronauts couldn't fix it because they were already in space. What I'm writing here about repentance and reconciliation may seem to some like an insignificant piece. Let us deal with it now, so that it will not cause greater difficulty later.

We have the power in prayer to go into the heavenlies and fix whatever is not working right. If we do our part in intercession and repentance, God will do His part in bringing the victory and blessing.

CHAPTER 16

ZIONISM AND ISRAELI POLITICS

In A.D. 70, the temple in Jerusalem and the nation of Israel were destroyed by the Roman army under Titus. These events began the great exile that lasted until the nation of Israel was established again in 1948. The exile and regathering of the Jewish people are major themes in the prophecies of the Bible.

In the generation following the destruction of the temple, new messianic hopes arose among the religious zealots who remained. The famous Rabbi Akiva eventually declared a man by the name of Bar Kochba to be the messiah. Under Akiva's spiritual guidance, Bar Kochba started a revolt against the Romans. This "Great Revolt" had disastrous effects, and was finally crushed by the Romans in A.D. 135. The exile and destruction of the nation were complete.

It is difficult for most Christians to understand the magnitude of this disaster upon the Jewish people, both nationally and religiously. Major sections of the Bible, including Second Kings, Second Chronicles, Jeremiah, Ezekiel, and Daniel, deal with the first exile to Babylon, which lasted 70 years. The second and greater exile lasted almost two thousand years.

Adaptations for Survival

The psychological trauma of this exile has deeply impacted our people. The religious expectations that Israel would bring the Kingdom of God were shattered.

Hebrew ceased to be the daily spoken language of our people. Each group of Jews began to speak the language of the country to which they were exiled. Hebrew became the language for religious studies alone. Without a spoken language, the rabbis were forced to canonize the basic prayers into a written liturgy that eventually became the "siddur," the Jewish prayer book.

The teachings of the rabbis, which had been passed verbally from generation to generation, also were jeopardized. Judah HaNasi had the oral traditions of the rabbis edited and codified into the Mishnah (completed shortly after A.D. 200).

After that, the teachings of the rabbis were primarily commentary on what was written in the Mishnah. Those commentaries on the Mishnah were in turn edited and codified into the Gemara (finished between A.D. 450 and 500). The Mishnah and the Gemara together form the Talmud—the encyclopedic compendium of early rabbinic teachings (containing over two and one-half million words).

In the mid-seventh century, Islam spread across the Middle East. By this time the Jews were scattered across both the Middle East and Europe. The spread of Islam divided the Jewish people into two major camps: Those within Catholic Europe and those within Islamic Middle East. That difference is seen even in Israel today between the Ashkenazic (European background) and Sephardic, or Mizrachi, (Middle Eastern background).

[Note: the word Ashkenazi in Hebrew means German; Sephardic means Spanish; Mizrachi means Eastern.]

Spanish Jewry

The Islamic empire reached into southern Spain. The Spanish Islamic culture was quite developed. There were ongoing clashes with the Spanish Catholics in the north. Eventually Spain was united under the Catholic monarchs. In Spain, both under Islamic rule and Catholic rule, the Jews lived well.

By the fifteenth century, the Jews had risen to such a high level within Spanish society that a backlash of resentment started against them. At that time, the overly zealous Catholic priesthood determined to convert the Jews by force. Some of those Jews who were force-converted, the Marranos, maintained Jewish traditions in their homes.

The priesthood became worried that so many "false Christians" would pollute the Church of Spain. In order to protect the purity of blood ("pureza de sangre") within the Church, they started a special court, called the Inquisition, to investigate the false believers.

The jurisdiction of the Inquisition was only within the membership of the Catholic Church in Spain. They investigated only those who had been baptized (despite the strange logic of baptizing people by force and then investigating them for being false believers). The Inquisition was not, by definition, an attack on Jews, but rather an attack on "judaizing" within the Church. [It is likely that among the Marranos were also Jews who were real believers in Yeshua, who wanted to maintain their Jewish identity.]

The Inquisition turned to increasingly harsher means of interrogation until it reached all-out torture. As the Inquisition failed, the exasperated monarchy and priesthood finally decided to expel all the Jews from Spain. In an amazing quirk of destiny and history, the Jews were required to leave Spain on the same day that Columbus set sail to the "Indies" in 1492. The prominence of the Jewish community in Spain, and its subsequent exile, gave the Jews in the Middle East and South America the name Sephardic.

[In 1588, the British wiped out the major part of the Spanish naval forces, following a sudden storm at sea, in the famous battle known as the "Defeat of the Spanish Armada."]

Luther and the Reformation

In 1455 a German named Gutenberg invented the printing press. By the end of the 1400s, over one thousand presses were operating in Europe. The first book to be printed was the "Gutenberg Bible." The printing press ultimately paved the way for the Bible to be made available to anyone who wanted to read it. Until that time, the Bible was in the hands of the clerics, and the common people had no direct access to the texts.

Within one hundred years, a religious revolution, known as the Protestant Reformation, took place. Its most influential leader was Martin Luther. One of the fundamental principles of the Reformation was that spiritual authority was to be established by the Scriptures, not by the priesthood. In 1517 Martin Luther tacked his famous 95 theses on the door of the Wittenberg church in Germany.

Luther was convinced that the reason the Jewish people had not come to believe in Yeshua was that they had been exposed to a false Christianity. He started out with a great hope that the Jewish people would come to faith if they could be shown the truth of the gospel directly from the Scriptures.

After years of having his message rejected by the Jews in Germany, Luther turned bitter against them. His later writings contained anti-Jewish statements, which were contrary to his earlier, positive attitude toward the Jews. Unfortunately that anti-Jewish sentiment in Luther's later writings became a seed of anti-Semitism in the German church, which later was perverted, and erupted into the pagan genocide of the Nazis.

However, the supposition is true, that if the Scriptures could be made available to all men, eventually the Jewish people would come to faith in Yeshua. That is happening in our day. In addition, Bible-believing Christians would be able to read about the purposes of Israel and be reconciled to the Jewish people.

Since the gentile Christians would have access to the Scriptures first, their reconciliation toward the Jews would precede and be the catalyst for the Jewish people coming to faith. That's why Romans 11:25-26 says that gentile believers should not be "wise in your own opinion" concerning the spiritual blindness that has happened in part to Israel. The proper attitude of Gentiles toward Jews will lead to the time when "all Israel will be saved."

Early Zionists and Ben Yehuda

By the mid 1600s, the awareness of the role of Israel had already taken root among the Puritans in England and the Pilgrims in America. The identification with Israel became so strong that the early settlers in Massachusetts almost named the colony, "New Israel." At the height of the British Empire in the 1870s, the Prime Minister of England was a Jewish Christian by the name of Benjamin Disraeli. Disraeli even wrote about his vision that one day the nation of Israel would be restored and become the spiritual center of the world.

Also in the mid 1800s, the modern concept of Zionism began to take root among the Jewish people. The concept of the return to Zion had always been present in rabbinic literature and Jewish prayers. However, that restoration was seen as something that would take place only at the intervention of God at the coming of the Messiah. It was not seen as a current biblical promise that could be acted on in a practical way.

At that time (the mid 1800s), the land of Israel was completely desolate. The famous American writer, Mark Twain, traveled to the Holy Land in the 1860s and described it in poetic detail as a complete wasteland. There was no major population in the country, except for a small number of Arab farmers and a small number of religious Jews. The increase in population, of both Arabs and Jews, began in the 1880s.

The first wave of immigration to Israel (or "Aliyah") took place in 1881. Among those first immigrants was a man named Eliezer Ben Yehuda, who believed he had received a vision from God to restore the Hebrew language. He heard a voice telling him to restore, "the language of the prophets in the land of the prophets." He took a vow to speak only Hebrew in his home. His son, Ben-Zion, is known as the first person in modern times to speak Hebrew as his native tongue. Strangely enough, Ben Yehuda was met with bitter opposition by the older ultra-orthodox community in Jerusalem, who saw his efforts at restoring Hebrew as a modern language as a "blasphemy of the holy."

Ben Yehuda was born in Lithuania. Educated in traditional Jewish religious studies in his childhood, he later received a more "Western" secular education as well. He and the other early Zionists were greatly influenced by the national liberation movements that were sweeping across Europe. They struggled with the question as to what kind of national liberation would be appropriate for the Jewish people. They concluded that the only possibility was a return to the land of Israel.

National Liberation and Theodore Herzl

The first national liberation was the American War of Independence in 1776, when America threw off the yoke of the British monarchy. Then followed the French revolution in 1789. After that the idea of national liberation spread throughout Europe and eventually touched the Jews living there. When the concept of national liberation, started by Bible-believing Christians in America, reached the Jews of Europe, it took the form of Zionism. Zionism is the national liberation movement of the Jewish people.

Because the Zionists were primarily secular, they met with increasing opposition from the orthodox Jewish religious community.

In 1895, a full 14 years after the first Aliyah to Israel, a secular Jewish Austrian reporter, by the name of Theodore Herzl, was covering the case of the court-martialed Jewish French military captain, Alfred Dreyfus. Herzl was shocked as he heard the Parisian crowd shouting anti-Semitic slogans. From that moment on, Herzl dedicated himself to promoting the establishment of a homeland for the Jewish people in the land of Israel. He founded the first World Zionist Congress in Basil, Switzerland, in 1897.

Herzl dedicated most of his time to appealing to European heads of state to support the idea of a Jewish homeland. His diplomatic efforts had their greatest effect in England, and paved the way for the Balfour declaration in 1917, in which the British government declared its support for the establishment of a Jewish homeland in Israel. At the 1904 Zionist Congress, there was a bitter dispute over whether to accept a proposal to temporarily establish the Jewish homeland in Uganda, instead of Israel. Afterwards, Herzl died suddenly of a heart attack, at the young age of 44.

At the first Zionist Congress in 1897, Herzl predicted that though it seemed impossible, within 50 years the state of Israel would be formed. And so it happened. Although Herzl encountered rejection from European diplomats and opposition from the Jewish religious leaders, his zeal and flamboyance incited the imaginations of masses of Jewish people, particularly in Eastern Europe.

Socialist Zionism and Ben Gurion

A large wave of immigration of Jewish people into Israel started in 1917, in the wake of World War I and the Balfour declaration. At the end of the war, the British took control of the Holy Land from the Turks. The story is told that when the British commander George Allenby reached Jerusalem to conquer the city, he dismounted from his horse, saying, "There's only one Man who has the right to enter this city riding on a white horse."

Most of the leaders of this wave of immigration were ardent socialists. Their Zionism was mixed with the hope of a socialist workers' utopia in Israel. Many were of Russian background and were influenced by the Communist revolution in Russia in 1917. Their ideology of labor strengthened the early "kibbutz" movement, and changed Zionism from simply a spiritual center to a viable practical community. The largest political party in Israel until the year 2000 was the "Labor" party.

One of those who believed in Zionist Socialism was David Ben Gurion, who was elected as the director of the "United Workers Party in Israel" in 1921. Through his leadership in the various workers' organizations, Ben Gurion established the administrative foundation of what later became the government of the state of Israel—of which he was the first prime minister. While Herzl was the visionary of modern Zionism, Ben Gurion was the father of the state of Israel.

Two Prophetic Messages: Get Out

In the mid-nineteenth century, the Jewish people were divided into three major groups: The Mizrachi Jews, living in the culture of the Middle East, Arabic speaking; the Western European Jews, secular, living in the culture and speaking the language of the country they resided in; the Eastern European Jews, largest in number, living in the "Pale of Settlement" between the Black Sea and the Baltic Sea. They were Yiddish speaking and ultra-religious.

From the late 1800s until the beginning of World War II, two prophetic warnings were given to the Jewish people to get out of Europe. One was the invitation to freedom in America, the other the invitation to return to Israel. My grandfather, for instance, left Eastern Europe, as a black-coated, ultra-orthodox Jew, at the end of World War I, and headed for America. Others in our family left as well; most stayed. Those Jews who stayed in Europe, instead of coming to Israel or America, were decimated in the Holocaust. Those who left survived.

Why did most of the Jews not heed those two warnings or invitations? Why did they stay in Europe? Why could they not discern the signs of the times?

In the emancipation that spread across Europe in the 1800s, the Jewish people found themselves with new citizenship rights. The concept of civil liberties started with the devout Pilgrims in America, who wanted freedom of religious expression for their vibrant faith. Civil liberties then came to Europe, but the vibrant biblical faith was missing.

In Western Europe, Jewish people rose to higher positions in academics, medicine, business, government, etc. They reached a particularly high position in Germany. It was in Germany that the Reform Judaism movement started, a movement that removed many of the archaic Jewish traditions that seemed to cause social separation from the Germans. German Jews began to speak like Germans, dress like Germans, and eat like Germans. Judaism was reformed to meet a modern world, which espoused religious liberty and equality. From Germany, Reform Judaism spread to America as well.

In the 1900s German Jews were prosperous. Their comfort blinded them to the coming dangers, which should have been obvious. When the world economy crashed in 1929, the German people grew resentful against the Jews, and blamed them for the social and economic problems. By 1939, the situation exploded.

The conditions in Eastern Europe were different. The ultra-religious masses were basically poor. It was not secular comfort that restrained them, but religious narrow-mindedness. The rabbis attacked Zionism for being secular and ungodly; they saw it as the people taking God's will into their own hands. The religious leaders told the people not to go to Israel. So the majority of the Eastern European Jews stayed—until they were massacred by the millions.

Religion and Politics

In the late 1940s and early 1950s, there was a huge immigration to Israel from those who had survived the Holocaust, and from the Jews who were fleeing from Arab countries. The population in Israel mushroomed. Each group of immigrants brought their own worldview, their own culture, and their own religious views. From these various groups, the political parties in Israel were formed.

There is a saying, "Religion and politics don't mix." However, in the Middle East, everything is religion and politics. Each political party in Israel represents a kind of messianic hope—each one only partial in its understanding, yet all holding some aspect of the bigger picture.

Throughout the centuries, there was always a small community of ultra-orthodox religious Jews in Israel. Until the 1950s these groups were anti-Zionist. They fought the state of Israel in every way. After the Holocaust, however, their ideology evolved to being more positive toward the state of Israel. While they disagree with its secular values, most of them see the state of Israel as a place for them to live and practice their religious beliefs in freedom.

Now that they are involved in Israeli politics, the main objectives of the ultra-orthodox parties are to get money for their religious schools and to maintain a draft exemption for their children.

The religious institutions in Israel were established primarily by Ashkenazi Jews. When the Sephardi Jews immigrated, they were told that their kind of Judaism was second-class. They were forced to submit to Ashkenazi rabbis, yeshivas, and customs. From the Ashkenazi the Sephardi learned to wear black, which was not previously a Sephardi custom. (Not to mention that it is inappropriate to wear clothing from Poland and Lithuania in the desert climate of the Middle East.) The most powerful rabbi of the Ashkenazi orthodox in the twentieth century was Rabbi Shach.

The Shas Revolution

In the early 1980s one of the leading Sephardi rabbis, Ovadia Yosef, felt that it was time to reestablish Sephardi identity and autonomy. He had a star pupil, Aryeh Deri, who also happened to be a political genius. The two of them formed the Shas party (Sephardic/orthodox). Shas grew quickly to become one of the leading parties in Israel. At the beginning, the Shas party had the blessing of Rabbi Shach; later the relationship varied between competition and cooperation.

The wide distinction between the secular and the religious is not found in the Mizrachi, or Sephardi, communities as it is among the European ones. So when the Shas party was formed, many of the Mizrachi Jews voted for them out of ethnic identification, rather than out of ultra-orthodox religious beliefs.

Now there are two main ultra-orthodox religious blocks in Israel, one Ashkenazi and the other Mizrachi. Both wear black; both are called in Hebrew "Haredi." They anger the mainstream Israelis primarily on two issues: Their refusal to serve in the army, and the usurping of tax money for their religious schools. Army service and taxation are two heavy burdens upon the Israeli public. In many people's view, the Haredi have lost their moral standing because of their abdication on these two issues.

The Haredi believe that they are the only ones serving God correctly; it is their exact observance of the traditions that brings God's blessing on the nation. They believe they are the only ones truly obeying God; therefore, only they can bring God's kingdom.

The Kook Revolution

A revolutionary concept in Judaism was introduced by one of the most influential rabbis of modern times, Abraham Kook, who immigrated to Israel in 1904. Kook's worldview blended three elements: The traditional ultra-orthodoxy of the Ashkenazi; the mystic teachings of the kabala, with an active faith to bring in the Messiah; and a strongly pro-Zionist view of the modern state of Israel.

Kook believed that secular Zionism and the state of Israel were the first stage of bringing in world redemption ("t'chila d'geulah"). After the secular Israelis would build the material part of the State, then the religious would take over to bring spiritual renewal. His theology combined Zionism, Jewish mysticism and ultra-orthodoxy into a coherent messianic vision.

In Hebrew, the word for donkey is *chamor*, and the word for material is *chomer*, both from the same root. Kook said that the Messiah would come riding on a donkey—meaning that the religious community would utilize the secular State to bring about world redemption. Some secular Israelis see this idea as crass exploitation. However, Kook's theology has opened the door for orthodox Jews to become strongly Zionist.

From this blend of orthodoxy and Zionism has arisen another stream in Israeli politics—the National Religious. These people are noted for wearing colored knitted head coverings and normal clothes, instead of the black

garb. They actively serve in the army and pay taxes. Many of the Israeli orthodox today are "nationalist." The more right wing of the National Religious are those who have established the new settlements in the "West Bank"
territories (Judea and Samaria). They see themselves as the new standard-
bearers of both modern orthodoxy and Zionist nationalism.

Secular Zionist Parties

Most of the prime ministers of Israel have been from the Labor party.
Their strength came from the early socialist immigrants and from the dominant leadership of David Ben Gurion. They represent the mainstream liberal party in Israel. Their standing was weakened at the beginning of the
Intifada, in the year 2000, after the collapse of the Camp David accords.

The Likud party represents mainstream conservative Zionism. Its
roots were in the more militant Zionists who opposed the British mandate
from 1917 to 1948. Its spiritual father was Zev Jabotinsky. His disciple,
Menachem Begin, became the leader of the Likud party, and the first Likud
candidate to become prime minister.

The leftist parties in Israel believe that through liberal humanist values, such as women's rights, secularism, and civil rights for Arabs, Israel
will become a more emancipated society and thereby bring peace. Once
when I was teaching at an evangelistic meeting in Jerusalem, we were attacked by a large number of ultra-orthodox. The next day, one of the left
wing Knesset members came to express sympathy and solidarity with us—
not on behalf of our religious beliefs, but for our right to believe what we
want.

In the year 2000, the new Shinui ("change") party gained popularity.
It has taken two major positions: One, as a moderate party between the liberal Labor and the conservative Likud; and two, as reaction against the co-
ercion and corruption of the Haredi religious parties.

Shinui's leader, Tommy Lapid, is a Holocaust survivor who was rescued by Raoul Wallenberg (a devout Christian from Sweden who sacri-
ficed his life in providing passports for Jews to escape the Nazis;
Wallenberg is recognized as a national hero in Israel). Lapid has stated that
he used to believe in God until the Holocaust, but his God died in the flames
of Aushwitz.

The ultra-right wing secular groups round out the Jewish political
parties. Their viewpoint is basically that the only way to peace is through

military strength and settlement of all the land of Israel, west of the Jordan.

There are also several parties representing Israeli Arabs, which control a little less than ten percent of the Knesset seats at this time.

CHAPTER 17

THE QUR'AN

The Qur'an (Koran) is the "bible" of Islam—the authoritative text that forms the basis of faith for millions of Muslims around the world. The Qur'an contains the words of the supposed revelation of the angel Gabriel to Muhammad. It was probably written down by one of Muhammad's close assistants around the year A.D. 650, or shortly thereafter. [The word *Qur'an* comes from the same root as the Hebrew word *Qor'e*, meaning to read.]

As a Messianic Jew, I find the Qur'an quite interesting. The Qur'an is not inspired scriptures. In fact it contains dangerous mistakes that have caused much damage in the world. On the other hand, the book as a whole strikes me as Muhammad's response to the corruption he saw in Judaism and Christianity in the seventh century.

Unfortunately, Muhammad was not exposed to Western Christianity or even to orthodox Catholicism, but rather to fringe groups that had traveled to the Arabian peninsula. As a Jew and as a believer in Yeshua, I am surprised to find how much of the Qur'an deals with issues concerning Judaism and Christianity.

Attitude Toward the Bible

One of the sections of the Qur'an that deals most directly with Judaism and Christianity is the "Sura" called *The House of Amram*. [My study of Islam and the Qur'an is quite limited. I am not qualified to give a general evaluation of either the Qur'an or of Islam. I would like to deal here with the particular questions in this one section, which reflect theological responses of Muhammad to issues in Judaism and Christianity.]

In the first verse of this Sura, the Qur'an is described as "the book of truth that Allah gave to you, O messenger, to confirm the Torah and the New Testament which He gave in earlier times for the instruction of men and to bring them salvation." What is surprising about this verse is its obvious affirmation of the divine inspiration and authority of both the Law of Moses and the New Testament.

In the viewpoint of the Qur'an, divine scriptures are divided into three general sections: First the Tenach (Old Testament), then the New Testament, and finally the Qur'an. That Muhammad saw himself as the final messenger given the third great revelation by the prophet Gabriel is similar to the claims of the Mormons that Joseph Smith received a third revelation that completes the Scriptures.

The Qur'an, as the third and final revelation, is seen as the most complete and therefore most authoritative of the three. Affirmation of the inspiration of the Old and New Testaments does not seem to be well accepted in the world of Islam today. The explanation is that the books of the Bible have been corrupted; therefore, only the Qur'an can be trusted as accurate. However, from even a superficial reading of the Qur'an, one is struck by how much modern Islam has distanced itself from the text of the Qur'an.

On Divisions Between Jews and Christians

In verses 17-18 Muhammad says, "The Jews and the Christians who received the Book in earlier times were not divided amongst themselves for any reason other than jealousy..." Here we see Muhammad responding to the divisions that he saw among Jews and Christians in his generation. His discernment was that these divisions came primarily from a spirit of jealousy. There is some wisdom in that, and reminds us of the words of the New Testament, which state that Yeshua was rejected by the Jewish religious leaders of His day because of jealousy (see Mk. 15:10).

Muhammad then instructs his followers not to enter into arguments with Jews and Christians, but to dedicate themselves to Allah with a full heart. Note: The word for *full* or *complete* dedication comes from a similar root to the Hebrew word for *peace* or *wholeness*, which is *shalom*. The Hebrew *sh* sound often converts in Arabic to *s*. It is from that root that the name *Islam* is derived.

The House of Amram

In verse 30 Muhammad goes on to describe the chain of faithful men, starting with Adam, then to Noah, then to Abraham, and then to Amram. One should remember that Amram was of the tribe of Levi. He married Yocheved, who gave birth to Miriam, Aaron, and Moses (see Ex. 2:1; 6:20). Although most Jews and Christians would not include Amram and

Yocheved in their list of the top ten greatest believers of all time, it is certainly praiseworthy that this couple raised three children who all became leaders of the faith in Israel.

Muhammad goes on to describe how Yocheved prayed to dedicate her son to be a servant of the Lord. Then Miriam is born, and Yocheved is surprised to find that it is a daughter instead of a son. Therefore she prays for her daughter Miriam's offspring to be blessed by God and protected from satan.

Here the Qur'an makes a significant glitch and skips up 15 hundred years to the opening pages of the New Testament. Miriam is then pictured as growing up under the care and tutelage of Zechariah the priest (husband of Elisheva and father of John the Baptist). The Qur'an describes Miriam as living in a room on the temple grounds and being fed supernaturally by God (verse 33).

Birth of Yeshua

Miriam is then told that she has been chosen and sanctified by Allah more than all the daughters of men. In verse 40 angels tell her, "Miriam, Allah brings you good tidings of his word about the birth of the Messiah, Yeshua, the son of Miriam who will be great and the son of the Most High in this world, and in the world to come will be among those who are closest to Allah." These words are quite close to the words of Gabriel in Luke 1:30-32a: "Do not be afraid, [Miriam], for you have found favor with God. And behold, you will conceive in your womb and bring forth a son, and shall call His name [Yeshua]. He will be great, and will be called the Son of the Highest."

Also similarly to the New Testament, Miriam asks, "How will I have a son since no man has touched me?" The Qur'an goes on to reply, "Allah can create whatever He wishes, and if He has decided upon a thing, He says, 'Let there be,' and the thing becomes according to His word."

Muhammad was dealing on the one hand with a corrupt, pagan theology that portrayed Miriam as the divine "Mother of God," and on the other hand with rabbinic Judaism, which rejected Yeshua as the Messiah altogether. Muhammad's compromise solution here seems somewhat reasonable, given that choice. His response to the claim that it is impossible for a child to be born of a virgin, by saying that the same God who created the universe by His word could easily cause a child to be born, is also quite logical.

Yeshua and the Torah

In verse 44 Muhammad quotes Yeshua as saying, "I have come only to fulfill the Law (Torah) which is in your hand, yet I will allow to you part of that which was forbidden to you." Muhammad was dealing with the disputations between medieval priests and rabbis. The priests rejected everything having to do with the Law of Moses, and the rabbis had expanded the Law to an elaborate set of traditions, which were virtually impossible to follow.

In the midst of that confusion, Muhammad pointed to the fact that Yeshua Himself obeyed all the laws of the Torah and claimed that none of His teachings were against the law. (See Matthew 5:17: "Do not think that I came to destroy the Law or the Prophets. I did not come to destroy but to fulfill." Yeshua did not instruct His disciples to fulfill some parts of the Law and not others, but rather called His disciples to understand the heart meaning of the Law and to emphasize moral purity rather than ritual observance.) Muhammad's words were probably closer to the meaning of both Moses and Yeshua than what was being taught by the priests or rabbis of his time.

In verse 45 Yeshua is described as rebuking the unbelief of the people around Him, and then crying out, "Whoever is on Allah's side—come to me!" This is another typical mistake in the Qur'an of mixing up a quote from the Torah with the Gospels. It was Moses, after the sin of the golden calf, who said, "Whoever is on the Lord's side—come to me!" (see Ex. 32:26)

However, it is quite interesting to see the parallel between Moses' challenging the Jewish people who had sinned, either to come to him or to be killed, with Yeshua's challenge to the Jewish people of His day to come to Him and be saved. Yeshua's ultimatum to His people was not a "Christian anti-Semitic" attack on Jews. He was a Hebrew prophet calling His people to repent or face the wrath of God.

Miriam and Miriam

The mistake mentioned earlier about confusing Miriam the sister of Moses with Miriam the mother of Yeshua shows a major breakdown in Muhammad's understanding of the Bible. Yet I can't help but appreciate his connection between the two names. As many Jewish girls are called Sarah, Rebecca, or Rachel in honor of the matriarchs, so was the name Miriam popular in honor of the sister of Moses. There is a spiritual parallel between the roles of Miriam the mother of Yeshua and Miriam the sister of Moses. Moses was the "savior child" as a prefigure of the Messiah. Both Moses and

Yeshua were in danger of being killed by evil government authorities. Both Miriams were entrusted with protecting and watching over the child.

[Note: Miriam, the mother of Yeshua, is the fulfillment of the virgin maiden prophesied about in Isaiah 7:14. The rabbis have always criticized this prophecy by pointing out that the word for maiden or virgin in Isaiah 7:14 is 'almah, which does not necessarily mean a *virgin*. However, Miriam, the sister of Moses, was also referred to as 'almah when she was watching over the baby Moses (see Ex. 2:1-8), and was certainly a virgin at the time. The Miriam of the Gospels is seen as a spiritual fulfillment of both the 'almah of Isaiah 7 and the 'almah Miriam, the sister of Moses.]

Resurrection and Divinity of Yeshua

In verse 48 Allah says to Yeshua: "I will take you out of this world and I will lift you up to me, and I will separate you from the people who have denied you. And those who have followed after you, I will raise them up above those who have denied you." Here again we find a compromise between Jewish and Christian positions. Yeshua is given a high and elevated position in the Qur'an. What is missing from this passage is the report of Yeshua's death and resurrection. The resurrection of the dead is mentioned hundreds of times in the Qur'an and is a main emphasis in Islam. Therefore the omission here is a significant error and represents a denial of the death and resurrection of Yeshua.

In verse 52, the Qur'an states, "Yeshua is in the eyes of Allah like the first Adam who was made from the dust of the earth." This follows the general pattern of the Qur'an to see Yeshua in a very positive light, but clearly to deny any divinity. Yeshua is mentioned several times in the New Testament as being parallel to Adam in the sense of starting a new type of human race to be born in His likeness (see 1 Cor. 15:45).

People of the Book

Jews and Christians are often referred to as "people of the Book" in a positive way (verses 64, 68, 73, etc.). In general, there is a level of respect for Jews and Christians in the Qur'an that is not seen in most spheres of Islam today. For example, Muhammad says that if you give some people of the Book a thousand dinars of silver, they will return every bit of it to you. If you give others of them one dinar, they won't return even that (verse 68).

Here Muhammad was dealing with ugly disagreements between Jews and Christians, who had laws concerning giving and lending money, that discriminated against one another by claiming the other was not a "believer." Muhammad calls his followers to fulfill their basic financial obligations regardless of that affiliation. His view of Jews and Christians is that their spiritual origins were correct, and that some of them in his day were still following that pure faith, but that the majority of them were corrupt and apostate.

On the other hand, there are dangerous verses in the Qur'an that call for all those who will not convert to be killed. Christians and Jews may be allowed to live if they become second-class citizens and submit to Islamic rule, but this allowance is optional. Other passages call directly for the murder of Jews because of their resistance to the Islamic faith. Unfortunately, the less tolerant view seems to have gained the upper hand in our generation.

Abraham and Ishmael

As might be expected, Abraham holds a special place of honor in the Qur'an. In verse 60 he is described as a *hanif*, a true believer who was neither Jew nor Christian. Those who want to be true believers should follow in his ways. That discussion is similar to the New Testament position about Abraham found in Romans 4 and Galatians 3, and the Tenach in Isaiah 51.

In a typical formulation, the Qur'an declares that we are to believe in what was revealed "to Abraham, Ishmael, Isaac and Jacob..." (verse 78). What stands out here is the importance given to Ishmael. In other formulations the Qur'an simply states that we are to believe in what was revealed to Abraham and Ishmael, without any mention of Isaac or Jacob at all.

The prominence of Ishmael would be expected, considering that Muhammad himself and all of those whom he was addressing were Arabs. Muhammad stresses that his faith and his God were the same as that of the patriarchs. However, Ishmael takes the role as the primary inheritor of the faith from Abraham, instead of Isaac.

Racial Sensitivities

It is not a coincidence that Islam spread so rapidly among the Arabic nations. Their identification with Ishmael was never lost. Racial sensitivities are passed on from generation to generation, and play a significant role in determining a person's religious views. Part of the difficulty in the international conflicts in the world today go all the way back to the error of Abraham and Sara in regard to Hagar and Ishmael.

Arabs have felt a certain disrespect from the Jews throughout the centuries, and later from the Christians as well. Racism has its fears and hatreds on both sides. It was not a coincidence that when blacks in the United States began to express their resentment against the whites during the 1960s, they turned to Islam in greater numbers. Some of them began to see their Baptist background as a white man's religion. How careful we need to be not to let even the slightest elements of racial pride distort our faith!

Moving the Temple

The most holy place in Islam is the shrine of the ka'abah in Mecca. In some verses in the Qur'an, this place is portrayed as the original holy place, before the temples in Jerusalem. Verse 90: "The first temple which was appointed for the sons of man is that which is found...in the city of Mecca. It is the source of blessing...and clear signs were given about its being the holy place of Abraham."

This idea represents a bit of creative folklore, which gave Muhammad justification to move the site of the holy place from Jerusalem to Mecca. It also fits with the cultural picture of Abraham as a desert dwelling nomad, more closely identified with the Arabs than with the Jews.

Critique and Respect

Muhammad then presents an overall critique of Jews and Christians. Verse 105: "You, people of the Book, were the best nation of all the sons of men while you were doing what is right and good, turning from evil and believing in Allah. Had you continued, O people of the Book, in your faith, it would have gone well with you. But today there are only few of them who believe and most of them are sinners..." Verse 110: "There are some among them who still read the signs of Allah day and night and worship him and believe in him... They do what is right and good, turning from evil and competing with one another in good deeds."

This passage contains a measure of respect and a measure of criticism, indicative of the overall balance of the attitude towards Jews and Christians found throughout the Qur'an.

Islam Reflects Jews' and Christians' Sins

The quotations from the Qur'an in this chapter give us some sense of the spiritual root of Islam. Islam is a great danger to the world today. It has had disastrous effects on history, religion, and politics. Yet I cannot say that its origins are impossible to understand or even unreasonable. In some ways

Islam is an indictment of certain failures within Judaism and Christianity. Islam reflects back toward Judaism and Christianity, like a strange mirror, the two groups' own errors one toward another.

Christianity, instead of seeing itself as a positive continuation of the Old Testament faith, positioned itself as a second religion, which denigrated its relationship toward Israel. Islam then established itself as a third religion, which attacked Christianity.

Judaism, instead of accepting expansion of the faith to the gentile nations, formed a barrier of ethnic pride, which rejected the Gentiles and emphasized the Jews' own physical descent from Abraham. Islam then used racial prejudice, attacking the Jewish people, while emphasizing the physical descent of the Arabs from Abraham through Ishmael.

In other words, Islam has done to Christianity what it did wrong to Judaism, and done to Judaism what it did wrong to Christianity. Where the Church was "replacement" toward Israel, Islam was even more replacement toward the Church. Where Judaism was legalistic and ethnic toward Christianity, Islam was even more legalistic and ethnic toward Judaism.

A Palestinian Christian Viewpoint

Here are some comments on the Muslim attitude toward Judaism and Christianity from Salim Munayer, Palestinian Christian scholar and director of Musalaha Reconciliation Ministries:

"For Muslims, the Koran theologically is what for us is Yeshua…the divine Word. The Koran always existed on a golden plate with God, and Muhammad is the instrument of bringing it into writing.

"As far as we know, Muhammad did not have direct access to the scripture. Most of his knowledge came from heretical Christian groups and Jews. For example, his understanding of the trinity is Mary, God and Jesus. From the Jewish background, in the Koran there are Talmudic stories, like the story of Abraham destroying the idols in his father's shop.

"Muslims view the scriptures that we have today as not the true scriptures that have been given to Christians and Jews, but has a corrupted version that shouldn't be trusted. This accusation has been directed especially towards Jews and later to Christians.

"Muhammad had been exposed to distorted picture of Christianity. He had no contact with Western Christianity or even Orthodox Catholicism. Every verse in the Koran that relates to Jesus, was found to be taken from heretical Christian groups that ran away from the Byzantines to the desert. Some would say that they were heretical Jewish/Christian groups.

"Concerning Yeshua, not only do Muslims deny His divinity, but also there is a denial of His crucifixion. They say that Jews did not crucify Jesus; they only thought they did it, but God did not allow it. That relates to the Muslim concept that God would not let His prophet to be killed.

"However, there are many verses in the Koran that refer to Jesus saying, 'Blessed is the day that I was born, die and have risen.' It would require a much longer article to deal with the whole concept of those verses.

"Concerning Jerusalem and Mecca, in the beginning of Mohammad's work, he advocated prayer toward Jerusalem; but when the Jews of Medina rejected him as a prophet of God, he turned to Mecca. That is part of the main process of the work of Mohammad to Arabize monotheistic faith. In other words, this was the failure of the church to translate the Bible to Arabic and to contextualize its message for the Arab tribes.

"I perceive Islam as a heretical religion, as many others do. In addition to its being a false religion, the destructive aspect of Islam is mainly due to the lack of separation of church and state. Since 1918, when Muslims lost the Sultan, they have not had a centralized religious political leadership, and that caused chaos in different Islamic schools. Saying that, we should not underestimate how powerful socio-economic modernization impacts the Muslim people, and their response to it."

Spiritual Root

The sin of man goes back to its root at the fall of Adam and Eve. The root of Islam goes back to the story of Hagar and Ishmael. The current conflicts between Jews, Arabs, and Christians have been complicated by the sins of all of us.

I am saddened to think that the pride and corruption of Jews and Christians may have pushed Muslims away from the faith in the Bible. I am also saddened that throughout the centuries, the religion of Islam has turned into such a monster, when its origins in the Qur'an were more moderate.

How important it is for us as believers to watch out for financial corruption in our midst, to purge every bit of racism, to avoid the slightest hint of sexual compromise, to reach out to others in love and tolerance, to humble ourselves from every trace of spiritual pride, and to investigate every aspect of doctrine with intellectual integrity! We have no idea how great the consequences are, both positive and negative. Let us pray for a mighty wave of evangelism to sweep the Islamic world.

CHAPTER 18

THE ROAD TO ARMAGEDDON

"All roads lead to Rome"—so went the saying of Caesar's empire. In the prophecies of the endtimes, all roads lead to the second coming of Yeshua. The second coming of Yeshua is the Main Event. Since Yeshua's return takes place at the battle of Armageddon, it could also be said, "All roads lead to Armageddon."

The word *Armageddon* comes from two Hebrew words: *Har* meaning "mountain," and *Meged*, meaning "a bountiful harvest." Today Mount Megiddo is an archaeological site near the junction of routes 60 and 66 in the lower Galilee. At the foot of this mound stretches a wide, flat plain that extends to the city of Afula on the other side. This valley measures about ten kilometers on each side, approximately one hundred square kilometers. In the hilly and narrow geography of Israel, this large open area is somewhat unique.

As one stands beside this wide plain, it is easy to invoke fantasies of huge armies converging in an apocalyptic battle—something of Hollywood, part *Lord of the Rings*, part *Star Wars*.

There is also the agricultural image. The Megiddo plain makes for beautiful scenery, yet it is also rich cropland. God sees the battle of Armageddon as the final harvest. Although there will be horrible bloodshed, it is the decisive victory of the Messiah.

Joel 3:12-14

Let the nations be wakened, and come up to the Valley of Jehoshaphat; for there I will sit to judge all the surrounding nations.

Put in the sickle, for the harvest is ripe. Come, go down; for the winepress is full, the vats overflow—for their wickedness is great."

*Multitudes, multitudes in the valley of decision! For the day of
the Lord is near in the valley of decision.*

The entire Book of Joel deals with the coming of the day of the Lord
and the battle of Armageddon:

Chapter 1—tribulation and difficulties
Chapter 2:1-17—a call to the people of God to repent and intercede
Chapter 2:18-27—restoration of the land of Israel
Chapter 2:28-32—worldwide spiritual revival
Chapter 3:1-17—the battle of Armageddon
Chapter 3:18-21—peace and prosperity after the war

There is a similar pattern at the end of the Book of Zechariah:

Chapter 12:1-3—Jerusalem becoming the center of international conflict
Chapter 12:3-9—all the nations coming to attack Jerusalem
Chapter 12:10-14—a revelation of Yeshua to the Jews in Israel
Chapter 13:1-6—spiritual revival
Chapter 13:7-9—a time of tribulation
Chapter 14:1-15—the battle of Armageddon
Chapter 14:16-21—the millennial kingdom on earth

The prophet Ezekiel also describes similar elements:

Chapter 36:1-15—the physical restoration of the land of Israel
Chapter 36:16-38—spiritual renewal within Israel
Chapter 37:1-14—worldwide resurrection of the dry bones
Chapter 37:15-28—renewed unity between Judah and the tribes of Israel
Chapters 38–39—war of Gog and Magog
Chapters 40–48—the Messianic kingdom on earth

All of the prophets speak of the same "big picture," although different
ones emphasize certain specific aspects. In end-time prophecies, people
often get sidetracked on minor details. Let's concentrate on the big picture,
and make sure the major elements of our theology are consistent with the
same big picture of Yeshua, the prophets, and the apostles.

The Coming Conflict

All roads lead to the second coming of Yeshua. Spiritual movements
throughout history will find their culmination in His coming. Political conflicts will come to their peak at that great confrontation. All current events
are setting the stage for the return of Yeshua.

The coming of Yeshua takes place at the great end-times battle. That battle involves all the nations gathered against Jerusalem. Therefore, it can be said that all the events of history are leading toward the attack of the nations against Jerusalem. All the nations will end up at that crossroads; they will have to pass through that sieve.

Zechariah 12:3
In that day...I will make Jerusalem a very heavy stone for all peoples; all who would heave it away will surely be cut in pieces, though all nations of the earth are gathered against it.

Zechariah 12:9
In that day...I will seek to destroy all the nations that come against Jerusalem.

Zechariah 14:2a
I will gather all the nations to battle against Jerusalem.

This focal point gives us a key to understanding events in the world today. How does world evangelism affect the attitude of the nations toward Israel? Will a war with Iraq or Afghanistan have a positive or negative influence? Will a peace treaty between Israel and its neighbors be helpful or hurtful?

Let us consider a scenario of how current events in the Church, in Israel, and in the world could converge at such a dramatic conflict.

The gospel will be preached in all nations. Wherever it is preached, there will be upheaval. The gospel will bring a shaking to communism in China, to Hinduism in India, and to Islam in the Arabic nations. As the gospel is preached, a remnant of believers will be formed in every nation. As those remnants are formed, the forces of evil in each nation will attack them.

In the face of those attacks, the believers will have to grow strong in their faith. As systems of communication increase, so will the awareness among the believers that they are part of an invisible universal body. The end-times body of believers will manifest all the elements that were seen in the first century believers, as described in the Book of Acts. There will be zeal and holiness, repentance and the fear of God. Miracles of healing, deliverance, and supernatural protection will increase.

Israel will become more and more the center of international controversy. Everyone's attention will be drawn there. The general political trend will move against Israel. However, the believers in each country will find themselves identifying more with Israel than with the political stand of their own nation. Thus the issue of Jerusalem will become a rallying point of unity for the international body of believers. The shared identification with Israel will cause a mutual identification one with one another.

The Tension Builds

Before the second coming of Yeshua, there will be a period of peace and prosperity in Israel. Here is part of the prophecy concerning Magog:

Ezekiel 38:11-12,14b-16

You will say, "I will go up against a land of unwalled villages; I will go to a peaceful people, who dwell safely..."

To take plunder and to take booty... against a people gathered from the nations, who have acquired livestock and goods...

"On that day when My people Israel dwell safely, will you not know it?

Then you will come...out of the far north, you and many peoples with you...

You will come up against My people Israel like a cloud, to cover the land. It will be in the latter days that I will bring you against My land..."

This peace and prosperity in Israel represents a major change from the present condition. There will be a war, a surprise victory, and a major turn of events. A peace treaty will be signed. Immediately following that time, Israel will experience rapid financial growth.

Many will see the victory in that war as the fulfillment of the battle of Armageddon and the peace that follows as the beginning of the Messiah's kingdom. However, that will only give a false sense of security leading up to the big war a few years later. The situation will be similar to the great victory of the 1967 war in Israel and the following over confidence, which set the stage for the disastrous Yom Kippur war in 1973.

There will also be changes within the country. A temple will be rebuilt in Jerusalem before the Second Coming. For a temple to be rebuilt, there will have to be a radical change of status on the Temple Mount.

Revelation 11:1-2

Then I was given a reed like a measuring rod. And the angel stood, saying, "Rise and measure the temple of God, the altar and those who worship there.

But leave out the court which is outside the temple, and do not measure it, for it has been given to the Gentiles. And they will tread the holy city underfoot for forty-two months.

Both the prosperity of Israel and the rebuilt temple become points of resentment among the nations in the area. At one point close to the Second Coming, an international coalition will take sovereignty over the Temple Mount area.

Within Israel, the peace, the prosperity, and the temple will be seen as signs of the coming of the Messiah. Messianic expectations will reach a fevered pitch. An orthodox rabbi will become head of the government. He will claim that since he has brought peace, prosperity, and the temple, he must be the Messiah. Thousands will follow him. This deception will be difficult to disprove. They will claim that Yeshua brought neither peace, nor prosperity, nor a temple. Therefore, there is more evidence for this man to be considered the Messiah than Yeshua.

Peace is the dream of the secular Israelis. Rebuilding the temple is the dream of the religious Jews. Therefore this false messiah will be able to gather the support of both sides of Israeli society. In that way, he will claim to have fulfilled the unity of the two sticks from Ezekiel 37. Despite the success of the false messiah, the movement of Jewish believers in Yeshua in Israel will continue to grow. That phenomenon will anger both the religious and the secular. Persecution will increase against the believers within Israel, just as it will increase against believers in all nations.

The trend toward globalization will give more and more power to the United Nations. Laws will be passed concerning environmental protection, human rights, anti-proliferation of nuclear weapons, etc. Israel will be an irritation to the nations, and sanctions will be brought against her. Israel will try to cooperate. There will seem to be great acceptance of Israel on some levels, but the deep resentment will remain.

Evangelical Christians around the world will be marked as fanatics and religious bigots, enemies of the spirit of international humanism. As the one-world government gains stronger control, believers will find their evangelistic activities labeled as illegal. As economic conditions around the world grow worse, the United Nations will try to impose banking reforms and a unified monetary system.

Gradually the utopian plans will go sour. The international government will turn into a world dictatorship. The false messianic society within Israel will also experience problems. The international dictatorship and the Israeli messianic government will find themselves sometimes in cooperation and sometimes in opposition.

The world government will declare a takeover of American finances. America's cultural and financial dominion will crumble. Western liberal humanistic society as a whole will begin to collapse. It will feel as though the "Dark Ages" are coming again.

As economic conditions around the world grow worse, so will the oppression of the one-world government. Persecution against Christians will intensify. The smoldering resentment against Israel for her prosperity, her role in the international community, and her claims of religious sovereignty will start to boil over.

Evangelism around the world will continue. There will be miraculous signs and wonders. Millions will come to faith. A grass roots revival will touch every nation. The end-times harvest of souls will be enormous.

At this point, the situation will begin to erupt. Scripture states that the world government will become a dictatorship and being a believer will become anathema—most likely a capital offense crime. The dictatorship will take full control of the Temple Mount. Israel will suffer open antagonism, as she is likely to be blamed for the economic problems of the world and accused of being racist. Tensions will steadily increase for a period of three and one-half years.

The Battle

After this three-and-one-half-year period, the situation will explode. From Scripture, we see that a united military coalition will launch a massive attack against Jerusalem. As Israel begins to lose the war, half of Jerusalem will be captured.

Zechariah 14:2

...the city shall be taken...

At that moment Yeshua will break forth with His angelic army from Heaven.

Revelation 19:11,14

I saw heaven opened, and behold, a white horse. And He who sat on him was called Faithful and True, and in righteousness He judges and makes war.

And the armies in heaven, clothed in fine linen, white and clean, followed Him on white horses.

Yeshua's armies will descend to fight against the coalitions of nations that have attacked Jerusalem.

Zechariah 14:3

Then the Lord will go forth and fight against those nations, as He fights in the day of battle.

With Yeshua will come not only angels, but also resurrected and raptured saints.

Zechariah 14:5

...Thus the Lord my God will come and all the saints with [Him].

As He descends, a fire will go forth from Him, similar to a nuclear power. The very flesh of those who came to fight against Jerusalem will dissolve. They will become instant skeletons.

Zechariah 14:12

And this shall be the plague with which the Lord will strike all the people who fought against Jerusalem: Their flesh shall dissolve while they stand on their feet, their eyes shall dissolve in their sockets, and their tongues shall dissolve in their mouths.

As soon as the war breaks out, the false messianic hopes of the Israeli religious community will collapse. In panic, they will search for any other possible solution. There will be no other alternative but one. During the three and one-half years leading up to the war, thousands of Israelis will have turned to faith in Yeshua. The religious leaders will have become jealous and angry. Yet the revival will continue.

As Jerusalem begins to fall, even the religious and government leaders in Israel will turn to Yeshua. They will cry out for salvation (see Joel 2:32), and in desperation invite Him to come as the Messianic King. They will declare, "Blessed is He who comes in the name of the Lord!" (Psalm 118:26a).

As Yeshua descends, His feet will touch down on the Mount of Olives.

Zechariah 14:4a

And in that day His feet will stand on the Mount of Olives, which faces Jerusalem on the east.

Earthquakes will occur throughout the world. The same fire that shoots out from Heaven will not only destroy the armies that attack Jerusalem, but will also transform the bodies of the believers and sweep them into the air.

1 Corinthians 15:51-52

Behold, I tell you a mystery: We shall not all sleep, but we shall all be changed,

In a moment, in the twinkling of an eye, at the last trumpet. For the trumpet will sound, and the dead will be raised incorruptible, and we shall be changed.

The last trumpet will sound. Not only will the believers be transformed and raptured, but the dead will be resurrected.

1 Thessalonians 4:16-17

For the Lord Himself will descend from heaven with a shout, with the voice of an archangel, and with the trumpet of God. And the dead in Christ will rise first.

Then we who are alive and remain shall be caught up together with them in the clouds to meet the Lord in the air.

The war will have been so large that it will take seven years to go out and collect the weapons that were used and convert them to civilian energy use (see Ezek. 39:9). From that moment on, Yeshua will begin to establish His kingdom government on the earth.

The Millennial Kingdom

After the war at the Second Coming, there will be a period of peace and prosperity on the earth lasting one thousand years. During that time, the devil will be locked in a special jail.

Revelation 20:2-3

He laid hold of...Satan, and bound him for a thousand years;

And he cast him into the bottomless pit... so that he should deceive the nations no more till the thousand years were finished.

During the thousand years, the martyrs and those believers who have been selected to serve in the first resurrection, will become a ruling coalition with Yeshua to govern in the millennial kingdom.

Revelation 20:5-6
The rest of the dead did not live again until the thousand years were finished. This is the first resurrection.

Blessed and holy is he who has part in the first resurrection... they shall be priests of God and of Christ, and shall reign with Him a thousand years.

During that thousand years, the international peace that was the dream of the Hebrew prophets will come to pass.

Isaiah 2:4b
They shall beat their swords into plowshares, and their spears into pruning hooks; nation shall not lift up sword against nation, neither shall they learn war anymore.

Not only will there be peace, but prosperity as well.

Micah 4:4a
Everyone shall sit under his vine and his fig tree, and no one will make them afraid.

The vine and the fig tree were the symbols of prosperity in the time of King Solomon (see 1 Kings 4:25). [The vine is also a symbol of the Church, while the fig tree is a symbol of Israel. During the millennial reign, the Church and Israel begin their mutual destiny. The vine and the fig tree will blossom together (see Joel 2:22).]

Jerusalem will become the central place of worship in the world. Yeshua will be there. The nations of the world will come to worship Him and to keep the feasts of ancient Israel.

Zechariah 14:16-17
Everyone who is left of all the nations which came against Jerusalem shall go up from year to year to worship the King, the Lord of hosts, and to keep the Feast of Tabernacles.

And...whichever of the families of the earth do not come up to Jerusalem to worship the King, the Lord of hosts, on them there will be no rain.

The prophet Ezekiel describes in detail the worship system that will be found in that Messianic kingdom:

- Chapter 40—A temple is rebuilt with courts and gates, and even tables for preparing the sacrifices.
- Chapter 41—The measurements are given for the sanctuary, the walls, and the temple area.
- Chapter 42—The various chambers for the priests are described.
- Chapter 43—Specific instructions are given for the building of the sacrificial altar.
- Chapter 44—A special class of righteous priests, called the Sons of Zadok, are described as ministering in that temple.
- Chapter 45—A large section of land around the temple is given to a special messianic figure called "the Prince."
- Chapter 46—This Prince will govern and lead the worship in the kingdom.
- Chapter 47—The desert is revived to a land of flowing rivers.
- Chapter 48—The land is restored in a conquest much greater than Joshua's.

Note 1: How could there be a temple worship system in operation together with faith in Yeshua? Don't we already have atonement in Him? Yes, atonement is in the blood of Yeshua. Sacrifices are only a symbolic remembrance, in much the same way that the bread and wine of communion, or the Passover, is. In the temple in Jerusalem before A.D. 70 were priests who were born-again believers in Yeshua (see Acts 6:7). They understood that the sacrifices were symbols, while their actual atonement was in Him alone.

Note 2: Most of the population in the earth during the Millennium will be natural people who survived the great war. They will live in non-resurrected bodies. Those of Yeshua's ruling coalition will have resurrection bodies in which they will be able to appear and be translated to different locations at will (see Jn. 20:19,26; 21:14).

The natural population will have free will, and there will still be a possibility of sin. Since the government in that world will rule in righteousness, sin will be much less. Death is a result of sin. Since sin will be less, people will begin to live much longer lives.

Isaiah 65:20

No more shall an infant from there live but a few days, nor an old man who has not fulfilled his days; for the child shall die one hundred years old, but the sinner being one hundred years old shall be accursed.

The flood of fire at the time of the Second Coming is a parallel to the flood of water at the time of Noah (see 2 Pet. 3). The Millennium is parallel to the period after the Garden of Eden, before the flood of Noah. At that time people lived for several hundred years. Similarly, the natural people in the Millennium will also live for hundreds of years. The millennial period will reverse the process back toward paradise restored.

Yeshua must reign during the Millennium until all of God's enemies are placed under His feet. The last enemy to be destroyed is death. By the end of the Millennium, there will be no more death. Then Yeshua will deliver the kingdom back to His Father. At that time He will subject Himself under the Father's authority, so that God may be all in all (see 1 Cor. 15:22-28).

Yeshua's one-thousand-year reign on earth may be seen as a transition period from the condition that the world is in now to the condition that it will be in the perfect paradise after the Millennium.

CHAPTER 19

HEAVEN AND HELL

At the end of the Millennium will come another war similar to that of Magog or Armageddon.

Revelation 20:7-9a

Now when the thousand years have expired, Satan will be released from his prison

And will go out to deceive the nations which are in the four corners of the earth, Gog and Magog, to gather them together to battle...

They went up on the breadth of the earth and surrounded the camp of the saints and the beloved city.

This last battle marks the end of the Millennium and the beginning of the final paradise, just as the battle at the second coming of Yeshua marked the end of the present world and the beginning of the Millennium.

The Bible counts several periods of "new heavens and new earth." The Garden of Eden was one kind of heaven and earth. The world from the expulsion of Eden to the flood of Noah was a second kind of heavens and earth. The present world, in which we now live—from the time of Noah to the second coming of Yeshua, is the third heavens and earth.

2 Peter 3:5b-7a

The heavens were of old, and the earth standing out of water and in the water,

By which the world that then existed perished, being flooded with water.

But the heavens and the earth, which are now preserved by the same word, are reserved for fire.

The millennial period will be a fourth new heavens and earth.

Isaiah 65:17
Behold, I create new heavens and a new earth...

Paradise restored after the Millennium will be the fifth and last new heavens and new earth that are described in the Bible.

Revelation 21:1a
Now I saw a new heaven and a new earth, for the first heaven and the first earth had passed away.

At the end of the Millennium, satan will be released from prison. We can only presume that at his release, the release of other demons who have been locked up together with him will also take place. Why should this release be permitted?

The battle at the end of the Millennium constitutes a last test for the human race. Since there will be free will in the Millennium, it will still be possible for people to sin. Satan is released in order to see which people want to remain loyal to Yeshua, and which ones want to rebel against Him.

There is a second reason. Immediately after that war comes the final judgment, with eternal punishment or reward. Human beings have a natural difficulty understanding the concept of eternal punishment. To us it seems unfair and very harsh.

Therefore that battle is also a last proof for the justness of eternal punishment. The battle will prove that even after a thousand years in punishment, the recalcitrant will not repent. Someone who has hardened his heart against God will not repent, no matter what the punishment.

In any case, the judgment of God will be perfectly just and perfectly righteous. The last battle will also settle the question of whether a human soul who had suffered in hell up to that time would be willing to repent. The fact that the final judgment at the end of the Millennium comes after the extended incarceration in hell raises the possibility that God may consider that punishment as sufficient for some people, and then let them enter into the new heavens and earth. Since the Bible does not answer that question, there is no reason for us to take a strong stance on it, one way or the other.

Heaven and Hell

Hell is not the eternal dwelling place of the wicked. No, the eternal punishment of the wicked is *worse* than hell; it is the lake of fire. Hell is located in the center of the earth (see Num. 16; 1 Sam. 28). Hell is a place where people suffer horrible torment; they are fully conscious of their surroundings.

Yeshua described a rich man who was tormented in hell, calling out to Abraham to send Lazarus to comfort him.

Luke 16:23-24
And being in torments in Hades, he lifted up his eyes and saw Abraham afar off, and Lazarus in his bosom.

Then he cried and said, "Father Abraham, have mercy on me, and send Lazarus that he may dip the tip of his finger in water and cool my tongue; for I am tormented in this flame."

The man being tortured was aware, awake, and in pain. But hell is the temporary place of incarceration until the final judgment. At that time hell will be destroyed, and the ungodly will be transferred to a different place.

Revelation 20:13b-15
Death and [hell] *delivered up the dead who were in them. And they were judged, each one according to his works.*

Then Death and [hell] *were cast into the lake of fire...*

And anyone not found written in the Book of Life was cast into the lake of fire.

The ultimate destiny of every man is either eternal bliss in paradise or eternal torment in the lake of fire. The suffering in the lake of fire is even worse, if that can be imagined, than hell. Not only is it worse in the degree of torment, but also in its duration. It will last forever.

Revelation 20:10
The devil, who deceived them, was cast into the lake of fire and brimstone where the beast and the false prophet are. And they will be tormented day and night forever and ever.

It is not God's will for anyone to go to the lake of fire. It was not designed for human beings, but for rebellious angels. However, anyone who insists on rebelling against God will end up with the same judgment.

Matthew 25:41b
Depart from Me, you cursed, into the everlasting fire prepared for the devil and his angels.

The eternal dwelling place of the righteous, on the other hand, is a perfect world that has been prepared by God from before Creation. That paradise is the intended destination of all men. Although men may reject God's will, perfect paradise is the place that God desires for every person.

Matthew 25:34b
Come, you blessed of My Father, inherit the kingdom prepared for you from the foundation of the world.

The eternal dwelling place of the righteous is not Heaven. It is even *better* than Heaven. It is Heaven and earth *combined*. It has all the elements of Heaven and earth together, both material and spiritual. God and man will live in harmony. That perfect paradise is the "new heavens *and* new earth."

Revelation 21:3-4
Behold, the tabernacle of God is with men, and He will dwell with them, and they shall be His people. God Himself will be with them and be their God.

And God will wipe away every tear from their eyes; there shall be no more death, nor sorrow, nor crying. There shall be no more pain...

This paradise is also called the new "Jerusalem" which descends out of Heaven onto earth (see Rev. 21:2,10). The new paradise has streets of gold and gates of pearl. It is not a cloud, nor a dream. It will be a solid, material world. Your resurrection body will be able to eat and touch and walk and talk. You will have trustworthy friends and enjoyable activities (see Rev. 21–22). The best part will be the loving fellowship with our heavenly Father.

Why Eternal Punishment?

Why does there have to be an eternal punishment of fire? Why couldn't God just disintegrate evil people so that they would cease to exist? Why not a momentary annihilation instead of eternal torment?

Isaiah 66:24
They shall go forth and look upon the corpses of the men who have transgressed against Me. For their worm does not die, and their fire is not quenched. They shall be an abhorrence to all flesh.

In the world to come, people will be able to go out and see the torment of the wicked. The punishment upon the wicked also serves as a witness to the righteous.

Revelation 14:10b-11a
He shall be tormented with fire and brimstone in the presence of
the holy angels and in the presence of the Lamb.
And the smoke of their torment ascends forever and ever.

When God creates something, it is eternal. It cannot cease to exist. The souls of men and of angels, both good and bad, are eternal. If we have re-belled against God, we will have to bear responsibility for that rebellion eternally. Free will demands accountability. It is not God's will to un-create us, but to have eternal justice demonstrated through our lives.

As the love of God is eternal, so is the fear of God (see Ps. 19:9). Par-adise is the eternal demonstration of the grace of God. The lake of fire is the eternal demonstration of the wrath of God.

We will always have free will, even in paradise. The potential for sin will always remain. Eternally there will be the same conditions as there were in Eden before the Fall. God does not want the Fall to be repeated. We have a positive motivation not to fall into sin, because of the goodness of God. We also have a negative reason not to sin, because of the severity of God (see Rom. 11:22). The eternal witness of the lake of fire is the perfect deterrent to protect us from sin.

The punishment of the devil is also a demonstration of the power of God. God receives glory by demonstrating His power. That power and glory can be demonstrated in two ways, either by blessing or punishment. God will receive glory by demonstrating His amazing goodness on creatures such as us, who have found un-deserved grace.

Ephesians 2:7
That in the ages to come He might show the exceeding riches of
His grace in His kindness toward us in Christ Jesus.

However, God can also demonstrate His power by His ability to de-stroy His enemies.

Romans 9:22-23
What if God, wanting to show His wrath and to make His power
known, endured with much longsuffering the vessels of wrath
prepared for destruction,

And that He might make known the riches of His glory on the
vessels of mercy, which He had prepared beforehand for glory.

Either way, God gets glory by demonstrating His power—either by
punishing the wicked or by blessing the righteous. Every person and every
angel will end up being either a vessel of wrath or a vessel of mercy. God
would prefer that everyone be a vessel of mercy. However, if someone insists on sinning, he chooses for himself to be a vessel of wrath.

2 Timothy 2:20-21a

In a great house there are not only vessels of gold and silver, but
also of wood and clay, some for honor and some for dishonor.

Therefore if anyone cleanses himself from the latter, he will be a
vessel for honor.

It is not God who decides. It is we who are to clean ourselves. We are
to choose our own fate, for mercy or for wrath.

Rewards in Heaven

Among those who are being saved, there are also different levels of reward. When Yeshua taught on prayer, fasting, and charity, He said that if we
do these things with a pure heart, then we will receive reward in the world
to come. If on the other hand, our motives are not pure, our reward will be
canceled.

Matthew 6:4,6,18

Your Father who sees in secret will reward you openly.

The people about whom He is speaking here are "believers." This is
not a difference between being damned or saved, but rather a difference as
to what reward you will receive in paradise. Each time we do righteous
deeds with a pure heart, we store up for ourselves reward in Heaven. To the
degree that we act hypocritically, our rewards are nullified.

Since each action has a cumulative reward, every person will receive
a different level of reward in the world to come.

In order to be saved, we must receive forgiveness of sins by faith in
Yeshua's sacrifice for us on the cross. He who believes in Yeshua passes out
of this judgment and receives salvation (see Jn. 5:24). God does not seek to
damn anyone, but He who rejects the offer of eternal life has, in effect,
damned himself (see Jn. 3:18).

In the sense of being condemned, a true believer in Yeshua is not "judged." However, there is another meaning to the word *judge* that is not referring to damnation or salvation, but to reward and punishment. In this sense every believer *will* be judged.

2 Corinthians 5:10

For we must all appear before the judgment seat of Christ, that each one may receive the things done in the body, according to what he has done, whether good or bad.

The apostle Paul made this statement to born-again, Spirit-filled believers. He included himself in this judgment when he said, "we."

If all saved people will live eternally in paradise, and if paradise is such a perfect place, how could there be different levels of reward there? Let us examine four areas:

Position of authority—The world to come is a real society. Everyone will have a job. There will be positions of leadership and government. Some people will have authority over thousands (such as ten cities).

Luke 19:17

Well done, good servant; because you were faithful in a very little, have authority over ten cities.

Others will have lesser positions (like five cities).

Luke 19:19b

You...be over five cities.

Others will have no authority at all (like one whose portion is taken away).

Luke 19:24b

Take the [portion] *away from him, and give it to him who has ten...*

A greater position of authority will be seen as a reward. A lower level position will be seen as a punishment. Both will reflect perfect justice.

Magnitude of glory—In the world to come, we will live in resurrected bodies. These bodies will be glorified, meaning that they will shine with light.

1 Corinthians 15:39

There are also celestial bodies and terrestrial bodies; but the glory of the celestial is one, and the glory of the terrestrial is another.

The difference between our bodies now and our bodies after the resurrection will be like the difference between the earth (which doesn't shine) and a star (which does shine). However, there is another difference.

1 Corinthians 15:41b-42a

One star differs from another star in glory.

So also is the resurrection of the dead.

Just as there is a difference in the magnitude of light coming from each star, so will it be in the resurrection. Each person's body will have a different degree of light shining from it—some more, some less.

> *Proximity to Yeshua*—While everyone in the world to come will have access to meet Yeshua, not everyone will have the same proximity to Him on a day-to-day basis. John and James' mother once came asking a request from Yeshua.

Matthew 20:21

Grant that these two sons of mine may sit, one on Your right hand and the other on the left, in Your kingdom.

While Yeshua could not grant her request, He did affirm the fact that there will be a certain "assigned seating" at events in the Kingdom of God. As a citizen of Israel, I have general access to meet with the prime minister. However, only those on his immediate staff can meet with him every day. Only those with higher positions in the government can easily obtain an appointment with him. The degree of one's accessibility to Yeshua is considered a great reward in the Kingdom of God.

> *Heavenly "treasure"*—It is said about money, "You can't take it with you." That is not entirely true. Just as there are banks on earth, there is some type of "banking" system in Heaven.

Matthew 6:20

Lay up for yourselves treasures in heaven, where neither moth nor rust destroys and where thieves do not break in and steal.

You make a deposit in your account in Heaven by *giving* money to others. I doubt if there is an actual "currency" in the world to come. However,

there must be some kind of "treasure" that Yeshua was talking about. Whatever that "treasure" is, there must be different degrees to which we can
"store it up for ourselves."

An Issue of the Heart

When God judges our works, He looks at our heart, not the outward
appearance. Many great works in the eyes of men are nothing in the eyes of
God. And many deeds that are seemingly worthless in the eyes of men are
of great value to God. Yeshua said that the poor widow, who gave two small
coins, gave more than the wealthy, who gave great sums of money (see Lk.
21:3-4). She made a greater deposit in the heavenly bank because her do-
nation required more faith and love to give it.

So it is with many other kinds of works. A great evangelist may be motivated by worldly ambition and therefore receive little reward in the world
to come (see Phil. 1:16). Another may only "succeed" in giving one cup of
water, but thereby receive the same reward as a prophet (see Mt. 10:41). If
you are faithful in the little thing that God has put in your path, you may receive an enormous reward in the world to come.

It is not unbiblical or selfish to be motivated by rewards in the world
to come. It is wrong to be motivated by the honor of man rather than the
honor of God (see Jn. 5:44). It is wrong to be motivated by the carnal rewards of this life rather than the eternal rewards of the world to come (see
Heb. 11:25-26).

However, we cannot be pleasing to God unless we believe that He will
reward those who diligently seek Him (see Heb. 11:6). Behavioral science
teaches that rewards encourage behavior and punishments discourage. The
concept of reward and punishment, both temporal and eternal, comes from
God.

A Divine Rebuke

There will also be punishments among those who receive eternal life.
Any sin that is repented of is washed by the blood of Yeshua and erased. Yet
sin that is not repented of will be punished. Five of the seven churches in
the Book of Revelation received rebukes from Yeshua. I am not speaking
here of losing salvation, but of losing rewards; by punishment here, I do not
mean damnation, but chastisement.

The Bible speaks of Yeshua having a "rod" that comes out of His
mouth. This means that the primary chastisement of believers in the world

to come will be a firm and honest rebuke by Yeshua—which will be witnessed by millions on Judgment Day.

Yeshua will not give us false compliments or flattery. If we have disobeyed Him or led a carnal life, He will speak bluntly and authoritatively to the point. I would rather be burned with fire or receive a thousand lashes than hear a word of disapproval from the lips of Yeshua on "that day."

Luke 12:47-48a
That servant who knew his master's will, and did not prepare himself or do according to his will, shall be beaten with many stripes.

But he who did not know, yet committed things deserving of stripes, shall be beaten with few.

Receiving a few more or less beatings would not apply to someone who would spend eternity in the lake of fire. Therefore, this passage must be speaking of believers. The levels of punishment in the Kingdom of God are meted out according to the degree of knowledge. There is a frightening responsibility that goes together with knowledge.

[The issue of receiving greater or lesser punishment again raises the possibility that some people may receive punishment in hell during the thousand-year incarceration and then be released after the final judgment. However, again, since there is so little in the Bible dealing with that issue, it is best to leave the question unsettled at this point.]

There will be different levels of reward and punishment. Some will receive more. Some will receive less. Some will receive nothing at all.

1 Corinthians 3:14-15
If anyone's work which he has built on [the foundation which is Jesus Christ] *endures, he will receive a reward.*

If anyone's work is burned, he will suffer loss; but he himself will be saved...

We are saved through faith in Yeshua. That is our foundation. With that foundation, a person builds his life with a quality like gold or silver, wood or hay. According to the life we live, we will be rewarded or not rewarded.

The Urgency of the Gospel

There is an urgency to tell unbelievers that a day of judgment is coming where they will face either damnation or salvation. There is also an urgency to tell believers that a day of judgment is coming where they will face either reward or rebuke.

The message of the Bible is both a fearful warning against eternal punishment and a gracious invitation to eternal paradise. The difference between those options is what motivates us to preach the gospel.

CHAPTER 20

THE DOUBLE SHOUT

Many times Yeshua raised His voice—when rebuking religious hypocrisy, demons, and sickness. However, there are two instances in which He gives a full "shout"—one has happened already; one is yet to come. Here is the first time:

Matthew 27:50

[Yeshua] *cried out...with a loud voice, and yielded up His spirit.*

Mark 15:37

[Yeshua] *cried out with a loud voice, and breathed His last.*

Yeshua gave a great shout at the last moment on the cross, right before His spirit left His body. This was not the scream of pain that He undoubtedly gave when the nails of the crucifixion were hammered into His hands. Nor was this a whimper of defeat and surrender.

There was something special, even supernatural, about the manner in which Yeshua shouted at that last moment. The centurion on duty at the time took notice of this unusual shout.

Mark 15:39

When the centurion, who stood opposite Him, saw that He cried out like this and breathed His last, he said, "Truly this Man was the Son of God!"

Yeshua died on the cross on purpose, according to the predetermined plan of God, in order to break the power of death (see Acts 2:23-24; Heb. 2:14-15). It was an heroic, single-handed assault on the forces of hell and the grave.

This was a shout of attack, like a soldier shouts when he runs into battle. This was the shout of a victor, not a victim. There was a certain aggression to this. Yes, He yielded up His spirit, but that was a firm decision, an act of His will. It required effort, concentration, and determination.

When Joshua descended from Mount Sinai with Moses, he misunderstood the shout of the people. He thought it was the shout of war, but it was the noise of people partying with the golden calf (Ex. 32:17). Let us not mistake Yeshua's shout in reverse. This was the shout of triumph and war.

Psalm 47:5
God has gone up with a shout, the Lord with the sound of a
trumpet.

There is another time that Yeshua will shout—at the Second Coming.

1 Thessalonians 4:16
The Lord Himself will descend from heaven with a shout, with
the voice of an archangel, and with the trumpet of God.

The Second Coming is the launching of an all-out military attack by the armies of Heaven against the rebellious angels and against the armies of the nations (see Rev. 19; Zech. 14). He will shout at the head of His armies; He is leading the attack. Can you hear it? There is such passion in it, such anger, and such power.

Surely the mountains will shake, the dead will be raised, and the enemies of God will flee from before Him. Surely the seas will roar and the trees of the field will clap their hands (see Ps. 96:10-13; 98:7-9). Let us tremble before Him, for the King is coming. He is coming to judge the earth in righteousness.

His shout is like the roar of a lion. Yeshua is at one and the same time a sacrificial lamb and a roaring lion (see Rev. 5:5-6). He who died on the cross as a suffering servant is the same one who's coming back as a conquering King.

BIOGRAPHY

Keith (Asher) Intrater

Asher Intrater is a Jewish believer in Jesus who came to faith in his Messiah during a dramatic confrontation with the power of God in the mountains of Central America. He graduated from Harvard University, cum laude; received an M.A. from Baltimore Hebrew University in 1982, cum laude; and received an M.M.S. from Messiah Biblical Institute in Maryland in 1984. He served as elder, pastor, counselor, and apostle in the Washington D.C. area for more than 13 years and immigrated to Israel in 1992 with his wife and 4 children under Tikkun International.

God has particularly anointed Asher to equip the body of Messiah to understand issues such as the relationship between Israel and the Church, prophecy and end-times events, Jew and Gentile reconciliation, and faith and personal integrity. He has spoken at many churches in the U.S. and abroad, including National Church of God in Fort Washington, Maryland; Church on the Rock in Rockwall, Texas; Strawberry Lake Christian Retreat with Gerald Derstine in Ogema, Minnesota; Hansarang Bible College and Onuri Church in Seoul, Korea; and Vida Nova Congregation in Sao Paulo, Brazil. He was the founding pastor of El Shaddai Congregation in Frederick, Maryland.

Currently, Asher is involved in fostering reconciliation among members of the body of Messiah through his work as a board member of Tikkun International; as an Israeli representative of the Union of Messianic Jewish Congregations; and as a core member of Musalaha Ministry, a ministry that fosters unity among Arab and Jewish believers. Asher is currently working towards raising up an apostolic team to minister, in Jerusalem and Tel Aviv, to Sabra (native-born) Israelis.

Asher has served as interim director of the Israel College of the Bible (ICOB) in Jerusalem, and Secretary of the Board of Messianic Jewish Alliance of Israel. Asher is the coauthor of *Israel, the Church and the Last Days*, and the author of *Covenant Relationships*, *The Apple of His Eye*, *The Five Streams*, and *From Iraq to Armageddon*. He speaks English, Spanish, and Hebrew. His dynamic speaking style and fresh perspective of the Scriptures will encourage and build your faith as we prepare for the coming of the King!

Note from the Publisher

In some ways this book is still being written. Therefore the author will continue to offer ongoing prophetic insights into the coming events in the Middle East. You can attain his commentaries by going to his website at:

www.revive-israel.org
or
www.tikkunministries.org

KEITH INTRATER

Covenant Relationships

Covenant Relationships is a handbook on biblical principles of integrity and loyalty. It lays important foundations for congregational health and right spiritual attitudes. You will be drawn into a deeper understanding of the meaning of covenant and commitment to personal relationships. Topics discussed include: relationships; how a blood covenant works, financial accountability; discipleship; patriotism and political impact.

0-914903-71-3

Israel, the Church and the Last Days

Dan Juster and Keith Intrater

The last days is a topic of great controversy in the Church today. Does Israel still count? Is the Kingdom now or future or both? Does the Church escape, take over, go down or have victory? Is there a Millennial Age to come or is the present rule of the saints the Kingdom Age? This book presents a new perspective on the last days and deals with all these controversial issues.

0-7684-2187-X